WORLD REALITIES SERIES
Editor: Brian Crozier

"... I have thought it proper to
represent things as they are in
real truth, rather than as they
are imagined ..."
Niccolò Machiavelli
(*The Prince*, XV)

First titles:

De Gaulle's Europe or Why the General Says No
LORD GLADWYN

Chairman of the "Campaign for Europe",
formerly British Ambassador to the
United Nations and to France

The Future of British Foreign Policy
MAX BELOFF

Gladstone Professor of Government and
Public Administration, Oxford

Starvation or Plenty?
COLIN CLARK

Lately Director, Agricultural Economics
Research Institute, Oxford
Fellow of the Econometric Society

Author of:

POPULATION GROWTH AND LAND USE
THE ECONOMICS OF IRRIGATION

With Margaret Haswell:

THE ECONOMICS OF SUBSISTENCE
  AGRICULTURE

Colin Clark

M.A. (Oxon.), M.A. (Cantab.)
Hon. D.Sc. (Milan), Hon. D.Ec. (Tilbury)
Lately Director, Agricultural Economics
Research Institute, Oxford
Fellow of the Econometric Society

Starvation or Plenty?

SECKER & WARBURG · LONDON

First published in England 1970 by
Martin Secker & Warburg Limited
14 Carlisle Street, Soho Square, London WIV 6NN

Copyright © 1970 by Colin Clark

SBN 436 10010 X

Printed in Great Britain by
Western Printing Services Limited, Bristol

Contents

Acknowledgement

IN THE preparation of the first few chapters of this work, I have drawn heavily upon material which first appeared in *The Economics of Subsistence Agriculture* (Macmillan, 1967), by Colin Clark and Margaret Haswell. I wish to acknowledge my debt to Miss Haswell's research and to thank Messrs Macmillan for permission to draw on this earlier joint work.

Foreword

THE WORLD'S food and population problem has been bedevilled by partisan and political presentation. In this short book I attempt to present it in its proper scientific perspective.

There does exist in the world a great deal of hunger and malnutrition (particularly protein shortage), though to nothing like the extent sometimes claimed of half or more of the world's population.

The problems of bringing the fruits of the world's abundant productivity to those who most need them are political and administrative, rather than economic or scientific, and the author is not well qualified to write on them. Political, because it is in fact a very difficult task to persuade the governments of the countries concerned to admit that their people are in need, and to ask for help, or to permit foreign agencies to distribute food; and even when there are no political obstacles, the administrative task of distributing food through improvised organisations in remote areas, in such a way as to make sure that it reaches the families in need and is not intercepted by the avaricious intermediaries who prey on them, is one of quite exceptional difficulty. Mr G. B. Masefield's excellent little book *Famine* (Oxford University Press, 1963), written from his own concrete experience, shows just how difficult the administration is. It certainly cannot be undertaken by those who are not thoroughly familiar with the country, and its language and customs.

COLIN CLARK

1

Food Requirements

WE CAN get some understanding of the food requirements of the human body by comparing it to a car engine.

The first and most obvious (though by no means the only) requirement is fuel. Every bodily activity, vigorous or slight—and indeed also mental activity—uses up energy. But we also use up energy, albeit at a much lower rate, when we are resting, or even sleeping. Ours in fact is the kind of engine which cannot be switched off, but has to be kept ticking over. Even when lying unconscious under an anaesthetic, the regular operation of heart, lungs, kidneys and other vital organs has to be maintained.

In common speech, the word "energy" has now acquired a number of different meanings. Some people use this word to describe mental attributes and character traits. To scientists, however, energy is a precise and measurable concept. It is measured in units which are defined as the capacity to lift one gram to the height of one centimetre against the force of gravity, or to raise the temperature of a kilogram of water by one degree Centigrade. This in fact is the precise definition of a calorie.[1] Energy can also exist in the forms of chemical compounds, electricity, light, radio waves, atomic nuclei, and others. They are all, however, capable of being converted into heat, and their energy content can be measured in these basic calorie units. We can of course also perform the converse process, as we do when we use a steam engine or

[1] Strictly speaking this word should be spelt Calorie in order to distinguish it from the calorie, a unit one-thousandth of this size, used for many purposes in science.

an internal combustion engine to convert heat into mechanical energy. This process, however, is not so complete. A substantial proportion of the heat remains unconverted, in the exhaust gas or steam, or reappears in the form of friction in the bearings, etc. It is for this reason that calories, rather than units of mechanical or other energy, are used as the basic measure of energy. Generally speaking, we cannot either create or destroy energy, but only transform it between its different forms; though creation of energy from the destruction of matter takes place in the stellar universe and, to a limited extent, in our nuclear reactions. Such exotic forms of energy, however, have no significance in the feeding of mankind, which can only obtain its calories in the form of energy stored up in chemical compounds, starches, sugars, fats and others, in the foods which we eat. This energy is released in our bodies by intricate processes, which might be described as a controlled (and highly economical) burning of these chemical fuels by interaction with the oxygen which our lungs extract from the air, without which we could not live for more than a few minutes.

The end product of these chemical processes is a gas, carbon dioxide, which we exhale into the atmosphere, as do all other animals, birds, fishes, insects, etc., not to mention the carbon dioxide produced by fires, furnaces, motor cars, volcanoes and other sources. In moderate quantities it is harmless, but if it went on accumulating in the atmosphere it would kill us. It does not do so because plants, all over the surface of the earth and the ocean, take carbon dioxide out of the atmosphere about as rapidly as we put it in. They do this by a chemical process of extreme complexity, known as photosynthesis, which we can follow, but which—in the present state of science—is too intricate for us to imitate in our laboratories. Readers with some knowledge of chemistry will be interested in the structure of the molecule of chlorophyll (see p. 29), which alone enables all green leaves to perform photosynthesis, which itself can only be synthesised with great difficulty: and also the immensely more intricate process of photosynthesis itself (p. 4). This process uses incoming energy in the form of sunlight to enable the plant to convert carbon dioxide into starches and other energy-bearing chemical compounds, some of which we can eat direct, and some indirectly after they have been consumed by animals whose flesh, milk or eggs we consume later. All our food has to come to us by these processes. There is no other way by which the human body can obtain the necessary energy nor, so far as we can see, will there ever be. Science fiction writers who enable their characters to dispense with food by means of pills, electrical discharges, etc., just do not understand the quantity of energy which has to be injected daily into the human body, and the impossibility of short-circuiting the absorption process.

In order to run a car, it is necessary to spend a considerable amount on maintenance, on repairing or replacing parts which have become worn or defective. To do the maintenance work on all the muscles and organs of the body we need the foods known as proteins. In a new car little or no maintenance is required. But here our analogy fails us. New

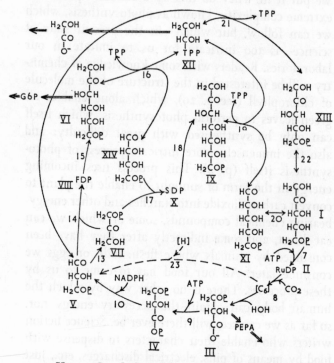

Key to Symbols in Photosynthesis Diagram

I. ribulose 5 phosphate (RU5P).
II. ribulose 1·5 diphosphate (RUDP).
III. 3 phosphoglyceric acid (PGA).
IV. phosphoryl 3 phosphoglyceric acid.
V. 3 phosphoglyceraldehyde (GA3P).
VI. fructose 6 phosphate (F6P).
VII. dihydroxyacetone phosphate (DHAP).
VIII. fructose 1·6 diphosphate (FDP).
IX. sedoheptulose 7 phosphate (S7P).
X. sedoheptulose 1·7 diphosphate (SDP).
XI. ribose 5 phosphate (R5P).
XII. thiamine pyrophosphate glycolaldehyde addition compound (TPP–CHOH–CH₂OH), phosphoenolpyruvic acid (PEPA), thiamine pyrophosphate (TPP).
XIII. xylulose 5 phosphate (Xu5P), glucose 6 phosphate (G6P).

human bodies are not delivered in mint condition from a factory, but have to be grown slowly from infancy. The proteins which are needed for maintenance are yet more urgently needed for the process of growth; and children require much more protein, in proportion to their weight, than do adults.

The proteins are chemical compounds of quite extraordinary complexity and variety. Their original discoverer indeed gave them their name after the ancient Greek sea-god Proteus, who was able to change his form and shape at will. What the proteins have in common is that they all contain, in approximately the same proportion, the element nitrogen, which is not present in the simple energy-yielding foods, starches, sugars and fats. The muscles and organs of the body all contain nitrogen, and it is clear that this element plays a key role in the growth and maintenance functions. However, it will not do to assess the value of proteins simply on their nitrogen content. When protein foods are digested, they break down into a variety of simpler compounds, the amino-acids, which are then ingested into the bloodstream. Even the reader with no knowledge of chemistry will be able to see that these are com-

---

Enzymes:
7. ribulose-5-phosphate kinase; 8. ribulose diphosphate carboxylast (carboxydismutase); 9. phosphoglyceryl kinase; 10. triose phosphate dehydrogenase; 13. triose phosphate isomerase; 14 and 17. aldolase; 15 and 18. diphosphatase; 16, 19 and 21. transketolase; 20. phosphoribose isomerase; 22. ribulose phosphate-xylulose phosphate isomerase; 23. hypothetical reduction of PGA moiety.

From: *Harvesting the Sun*, p. 81, edited by A. San Pietro, F. A. Greer and T. J. Army, by kind permission of Academic Press Inc. New York, who hold the copyright.

AMINO ACIDS THAT COMMONLY
OCCUR IN PROTEINS

LYSINE

$$NH_2 - CH - CO_2H$$

with $(CH_2)_4 - NH_2$ attached to the CH.

TRYPTOPHAN

$$NH_2 - CH - CO_2H$$

METHIONINE

$(CH_2)_2 - SCH_3$

$$NH_2 - CH - CO_2H$$

From 'Biological Chemistry' by H. R. Mahler
and E. H. Cordes

pounds of comparatively simple structure, some of which can in fact be synthesised, though generally at a cost exceeding that of obtaining them from natural sources. The amino-acids all contain nitrogen, but have differing chemical structures, and some proteins are known to be deficient in certain amino-acids which the body urgently requires. People living on a cereal diet may find themselves seriously short of lysine and tryptophan, but these deficiencies can be put right by eating a moderate quantity of legumes (peas, beans, etc.). If these amino-acids are in balance, the next danger of deficiency probably arises for methionine. This is present in vegetable foods, but animal proteins contain it more abundantly.

A mechanic repairing a car takes out any part found to be seriously worn or defective, and replaces it with a new part from the factory. The old part will be thrown away, or possibly may have some minor value as scrap. Although grafting of certain human "spare parts", including the heart, has been achieved we are not in general in a position to act like that. In fact, the process of body maintenance is marvellously economical. The amino-acids and other compounds circulate in the blood-stream, repairing each part as soon as it is necessary, but carefully carrying away the scrap to be used again in some simpler process. It has been estimated that each atom of nitrogen which we consume in our protein intake on the average engages in about four successive maintenance processes, until it has been reduced to one of the simplest chemical forms in which it cannot be used any longer, when it is excreted through the kidneys.

There is a nutritional counterpart of the lubricants of a car. In order for it to run, you have to do more than provide it with fuel. You have to provide it with a sufficient quantity of lubricant. Here in fact we have a fairly precise analogy. Different lubricants are required for different parts of the system. They are capable of being stored in the system for a time and do not require daily replenishment. They are needed only in small quantities, but extremely serious consequences ensue if they are neglected. The "lubricants" of the human body are the vitamins and minerals. It was shown by Hopkins in 1906 (though in fact it appears that one of the key experiments had been performed over twenty years earlier) that hitherto healthy laboratory rats soon sickened and died when fed on a chemically pure diet of starch, sugar, fat and protein; but that they could quickly be put right by very small quantities of fresh milk and green vegetables. The vitamins thus discovered, which are necessary—in small quantities—for health, are now known to include a considerable range of chemical compounds of varying complexity, some of which are comparatively simple, and can be synthesised if required. Some very serious diseases in the past have been shown to be due to vitamin deficiencies. These include scurvy, which took such a toll of seamen and explorers, pellagra, which attacked people living predominantly on maize, and beri-beri in Asia, which arose among labourers fed on rice with the outer skin polished off.

It does not follow that we should all consume more vitamins, as is sometimes suggested. Indeed, an excessive intake of vitamins may do serious harm.

Besides the vitamins, the human body has need of certain mineral elements. Calcium, phosphorus, iron and sulphur are needed in significant quantities for essential bodily processes. In addition to these, the human body requires a great range of inorganic elements in minute quantities—the so-called trace-element requirements. Some of these requirements are quite extraordinary—manganese for lactation, zinc for the development of the reproductive organs, silver for the lens of the eye. It is believed that, under normal circumstances, we pick up all we need in the way of trace-elements from atmospheric dust and terrestrial dirt; but circumstances conceivably might arise in which a deficiency of one of these trace-elements might have serious consequences.

We now turn to the examination of food requirements and food shortages, and the strange part in this discussion which has been played by the World Food and Agriculture Organisation, commonly known as FAO.

In the early years of the century, there was formed, with meagre support from the governments of the day, an International Institute of Agriculture, with its offices in Rome. With its scanty resources, this Institute nevertheless succeeded in bringing together the agricultural statistics of the whole world in one annual volume, and also in publishing two journals, for the international dissemination of new knowledge in the fields of agricultural science, and of agricultural economics and statistics, respectively.

In 1945, the United Nations organisation was formed. It took over the old Institute and transformed it into the World Food and Agriculture Organisation.

The expense of the new organisation has been out of all comparison with that of the old; but the amount of useful work done has risen in a much more modest proportion. FAO was sardonically described by *The Economist*[2] as "a permanent institution devoted to proving there is not enough food in the world". For a long time (although things have recently become very different under the new Director-General, Dr Boerma) the activities of FAO gave the impression of an organisation dominated by Public Relations men, with the dissemination of accurate information taking second place to their activities. It is true that in the years immediately after 1945 the world was faced with serious food shortages. The first Director-General of FAO was Lord Boyd-Orr, who had been a courageous army surgeon in the First World War, then a distinguished scientist who successfully treated some harmful sheep diseases. But his views on economics and politics were strange. He wanted all transactions in agricultural products all over the world to be controlled by a single international board, and was pained and surprised when the Labour Government of his own country doggedly opposed entrusting to any such board powers which would literally have enabled it to starve Britain into submission, a thing which Hitler never succeeded in doing.

On retiring from the post of Director-General of FAO, Lord Boyd-Orr published[3] the statement that "a lifetime of malnutrition and actual hunger is the lot of at least two-thirds of mankind". This extra-

[2] 23 August 1952.
[3] *Scientific American*, New York, August 1950.

ordinary misstatement (which is in fact based on an arithmetical error) still continues to circulate. People tend to believe that anything which they have heard so often must be true. It may indeed be a problem for social psychologists to explain how such a strange statement came to be so widely and passionately believed. Many people seem to be under some compelling emotional necessity to exaggerate the extent of misery in the world. Particularly blameworthy, however, are a number of eminent literary men, scientists and theologians, learned men who are expected to examine carefully the evidence on which all their statements are based, who nevertheless proclaimed this "two-thirds of mankind" story, and expected others to follow them. It did of course provide excellent emotional fuel for those who believed that the world was overpopulated, for those who believed that a world revolution was needed, and for those who combined these beliefs.

How Lord Boyd-Orr's statement came to be made constitutes an interesting intellectual detective story, which was unravelled by M. K. Bennett, Director of the Food Research Institute at Stanford University, and probably the leading world authority in this field.[4]

Bennett carefully scrutinised the text of FAO's *Second World Food Survey*, which was not published until 1952, but which appears to have contained the material on which Lord Boyd-Orr was working. This survey included a statistical table, for which neither sources nor methods of compilation were given, purporting to show average calorie

[4] *The World's Food*, Harper Bros., New York, 1954.

requirements per head of all the nations in the world, and comparing these with supposed data on calorie supplies—data which, for most of the countries in question, have not since been republished, because of serious doubts about their accuracy.

These very dubious calculations (which showed, for instance, that Portugal was seriously undernourished, but not Spain) nevertheless fixed figures for supposed calorie requirements well below FAO's earlier "estimates". But Bennett's examination of Lord Boyd-Orr's text compels him to conclude—"one cannot escape the inference"—that he had completely mixed up the statistics (inaccurate in any case) which had been placed before him; and had taken as supposed minimum requirements, below which people would actually suffer hunger, a set of figures of "targets" for production at some time in the future (which targets FAO itself had in fact already abandoned).

After some years, FAO came to realise that this statement was erroneous. But they did not wish to lose its emotional impact. Late in the 1950s they came out with the statement that half the world was suffering from malnutrition. FAO gave neither any evidence for this statement, nor even a definition of malnutrition. But they succeeded in getting it widely accepted, even to the point of persuading both President Kennedy and the Duke of Edinburgh to make speeches which were centred on this supposed fact. When asked for the evidence, FAO stated that it was still in preparation, and in fact years elapsed before they could produce it. (It appears that the original statement had been made just as a piece of public relations, without any evidence at all.) To heighten the irony, they had to borrow an expert from the Oxford University Institute of Agricultural Economics to help them prepare their case. When at last they published the grounds for their statement (in *Third World Food Survey*) it transpired that they were defining as malnourished anyone who did not eat as well as the inhabitants of France or Britain, i.e. deriving 20 per cent or more of their calorie intake from animal products, fruits and vegetables, and fats and oils. No medical evidence whatsoever was produced to support the assertion that this constituted the borderline of malnutrition. In fact, when one looks at the medical records of France and Britain, it appears that a good many of the inhabitants are suffering quite seriously from overnutrition, and these countries certainly do not constitute a borderline case of malnutrition.

Publication of statements of this sort is not only scientifically inaccurate, but has had other serious consequences. All over the world, particularly in Europe, there have been agricultural politicians agitating for higher prices and subsidies to enable them to produce more. When it is pointed out to them that this may lead to more production than their country's markets can consume, then the FAO propaganda gives them a marvellous escape route. "Is there not the starving world outside, which will be delighted to receive, either as a gift or at a nominal price, any surplus food which we may happen to produce?" FAO and the European politicians are now having to face the consequences of having followed these untruths, with quantities of unsaleable butter accumulating in Europe, and the prospect of surpluses of cereals and sugar soon accumulating as well.

It is quite true that there are many people in the world who are hungry, or near the hunger line, though nothing like half the world's population. But of the countries in which these hungry people live, some, like China, after purchasing a small quantity of imported food, decline to negotiate further with the outside world; many other governments will firmly deny that there is any hunger within their borders, and it is quite impossible to force food supplies on them in face of such a denial; at most there will be some countries like India and Indonesia, which will admit that they are temporarily short of food, but even so will only accept limited quantities of the foods which they, not their benefactors, choose; at the same time making it quite clear that they regard such arrangements as strictly temporary, and that it is their duty, which they will carry out within a few years, to make their own agriculture self-sufficient. All policies based on the idea of producing surplus food and then giving it away will prove unsuccessful.

FAO prepared a number of statements showing calorie requirements, averaged per head of the population, and then classifying countries as being at or below the hunger level. But their supposed standard dissolved in ridicule when the Australian anthropologist, Margaret MacArthur,[5] examining a large number of Japanese family consumption studies, showed that, if FAO standards were true, then a large proportion of the population of Japan was starving—and this in

[5] *Journal of the Royal Statistical Society*, 1964.

a country where the majority of families own tele-
vision sets. A study in Ceylon by Cullumbine,[6] which
FAO had used to support their case, in fact proves
the opposite. A number of Ceylon Tamil boys aged
8–15 were found to be consuming calories at a rate
of only a little over half their requirements, as hypo-
thesised by FAO. These were boys from comparatively
wealthy families, and showed no sign of ill-health or
lack of activity. Estimates of calorie requirements
for African children far below those of FAO were
were also calculated by Fox.[7]

The final argument against accepting the FAO
figures is the experience of China. The information
available indicates that for several years in the early
1960s calorie consumption per head per day in China
was only about 1600. This is below the estimates of
actual needs of 1800–2000 given below, and hunger
and suffering must have been considerable. (There
are some indications that things are better now,
although not by very much.) But if the FAO figure
for minimum calorie requirements of 2300 is correct,
most of the population of China must be dead by now.

To try to fix a single calorie standard for the world
is in any case quite mistaken. It does not require
much reflection to see that some populations contain
a much higher proportion of children than others,
which has a big effect on calorie requirements, when
we calculate them per head of the whole population;
and that men differ very much in the amount of hard
physical work which they may do. And even when
working at similar intensity, men of greater body

[6] *Ceylon Journal of Medical Science,* 1949.
[7] Ph.D. Thesis, University of London, 1953.

weight require more calories. The Swedish Forest Research Institute[8] compared the calorie consumption of men engaged in logging—about the most strenuous work there is—in Sweden and in India. The amount of calorie consumption per minute was 16·5 for the Swedes and 9·8–11·7 for the Indians, a figure almost exactly proportional to their relative body weights, of 72 kg. and 45–50 kg. respectively. Finally, calorie requirements are affected by climate— in a cold climate the body has to burn up a certain number of calories just to keep itself warm.

The calorie requirements for various activities can be precisely measured, if you can persuade a man to wear a close-fitting mask over his head, with chemical apparatus attached which measures the rate at which he is exhaling carbon dioxide, and consequently the rate at which he is using up calories—though it is difficult to persuade men to do this in tropical climates. The figure quoted above for Swedish loggers showed that a big man, doing the most strenuous work there is, in a cold climate, may be burning up calories at the exceptional rate of 1000 per hour. But even the strongest cannot keep this up for long. A certain amount of rest, or intermittent lighter work, is a physiological necessity. Averaged over his whole working day, it is estimated that a European manual worker, even if engaged in fairly heavy work, will only consume calories at an average rate of 300 per hour, though individual men doing unusually heavy work will average more.

[8] Hansson, Lindholm and Birath, *Men and Tools in Indian Logging Operations*, Skoghögskolan, Stockholm, 1966.

Under African conditions of temperature, body weight and methods of working, the calorie consumption of an able-bodied man is estimated at 250 per hour while he is engaged in work or active recreational activities, 184 per hour while he is walking, 78 per hour for sedentary activities, and a minimum of 62½ per hour (to maintain basic bodily metabolism) while he is sleeping. A woman's requirements are generally less, in proportion to her body weight, though raised by pregnancy or lactation.

How much of the day is spent in physical activities and how much in sedentary can unfortunately only be estimated within very wide margins.

A range of estimates can be made for the per head calorie requirements of African and Asian countries.[9] The high proportion of children in these populations must always be borne in mind, and for this reason alone per head calorie requirements must be expected to be lower than for a European or North American population. The range of variation starts from as low as 1625 for a small-bodied people in a hot climate— say South-East Asia—and not fully occupied throughout the agricultural year. At the other end of the scale, we may take a large-bodied people in a cold climate—say the Northern Chinese—working hard and continuously throughout the agricultural year, with requirements slightly over 2000.

Now let us consider the satisfaction of these requirements by means of grain, the staple food of mankind. The word "grain" is used advisedly to cover not only the wheat which we are accustomed to

[9] For full details, see Clark and Haswell, *The Economics of Subsistence Agriculture*, Chapter 1.

eat, but also the rye, oats, barley, maize, sorghum, millet and rice which are consumed as staple foods in different parts of the world.

As these grains grow, they are covered by various husks or outer layers. In the case of our wheat, we mill off not only the roughest and most fibrous outer layer, the bran, but also successive inner layers, all of which are sold for animal feeding, until we get down to only about two-thirds of the weight of the original grain (except for the minority who buy wholemeal flour and bread).

Such extensive milling, however, is more to provide for our taste than for our physiological necessity. Most of us now prefer white bread. But the fact that wholemeal bread eaters now, and all our ancestors until comparatively recently, have lived in comparatively good health, makes it clear that there is no physiological need to mill as much as we do.

Medical authorities, however, do not advise going to the opposite extreme, and eating all our grains complete, including the bran. "Bran is used industrially for polishing steel," said one medical professor, "why use it on your intestines?" Hungry tribesmen, who do have to watch every ounce of food, nevertheless still find it necessary, in most cases, to mill away about 10 per cent of their grains.

Rice differs from other grains in having an exceptionally large and tough husk. Even the hardy Japanese and Taiwanese find it necessary to mill rice down to about 73 per cent of its original weight, and some more fastidious Asians, who like their rice white and polished (at the risk of getting beri-beri), may mill it down to as low as 60 per cent of its original weight. In this respect, rice measured at unmilled weight is of less value than a similar weight of other unmilled grains. It is always necessary to be very careful of the definitions when we are looking at any information about rice. Supplies are often expressed at milled weight, in which case, of course, they represent a higher value than the same weight of other grains.

One kilogram[10] of most grains (other than rice), after the outer husk, to the weight of approximately 10 per cent, has been milled off and fed to livestock, will give on the average about 3150 calories of human food. A simple calculation shows us that an African or Asian population, if they are to obtain their calories *entirely* from grain, are going to need between one-half and two-thirds of a kilogram per person per day, or between 190 and 235 kilograms (under a quarter of a ton) per head per year.

At this point we may stop to consider protein requirements. Many people are under the erroneous impression that grains and bread, as carbohydrate foods, do not contain protein. They are mistaken. The protein content of grains ranges from 8 to 13 per cent. Even for a single type of grain, it is hard to state the figure much more precisely, because the protein content may vary considerably with the years, weather, land on which the grain was grown, etc.

[10] All measures in this book will be expressed in metric units. (Britain really should make an effort to get used to them before their day of legal requirement comes.) 1 kilogram is 2·205 lb. and a metric ton of 1000 kilograms is almost identical with (1·6 per cent less than) the old British ton of 2240 lb.

The study of calorie requirements is still rather an approximate science. But the study of protein requirements, in spite of all the scientific efforts which have been devoted to it, leads to much more uncertain conclusions. In contrast with previous high estimates, medical authorities now estimate protein requirements for adults at only about half a gram per day per kilogram of body weight, i.e. about 25 grams per person per day for an African or Asian population. For growing children protein requirements, per kilogram of body weight, are about three times as high. The average body weight of growing children, however, is probably a third or less of the average body weight of adults, and therefore total requirements per head should be about the same. The medical authorities, however, specify that, if you are consuming at these minimum levels, you require good-quality protein. Protein, it will be remembered, is very far from being measurable in uniform units, as are calories. The protein molecules themselves, of indescribable complexity, are hydrolysed by our stomach acids into the comparatively simple amino-acids, though even these are difficult to describe in respect of all their functions. Just to make the problem more difficult again, we may, under certain circumstances, have micro-organisms in our intestines, and under other circumstances not have them, capable of converting one amino-acid into another.

You can be sure of high-quality protein if you consume it in animal form, that is to say from meat, fish, eggs or milk. Of all these proteins, that contained in milk is the best—as indeed it ought to be, if it is to be the sole food of the infant during the first, and nutritionally most important year of his life. We consume most of the milk proteins when we eat cheese, though not when we eat butter, in the preparation of which nearly all the protein is washed away with the pig swill.

All the animal proteins are of high quality. But it does not necessarily follow that we *need* to eat them in substantial quantities. During the 1930s, not only were total requirements of protein put much higher than they are now, but we were also told that at least half our intake ought to be in the form of animal proteins. It was rather ironic that some of the physiologists who were telling Britain that the country was gravely undernourished in the 1930s, had to reappear as official apologists during the 1940s, when food supplies really had been substantially reduced, to tell the British people that they were adequately fed. It was at about this time that fat disappeared from the list of supposed physiological requirements. During the 1930s we were supposed to need 100 grams per head per day, i.e. 3 ounces, quite a substantial amount. Subsequently we have been told that the consumption of fat is just a matter of palatability rather than a physiological need, and indeed that a hearty consumption of fat is likely to be dangerous to the heart and arteries.

It began to dawn on physiologists, a little late in the day, that there are very large communities throughout the world who never touch milk or dairy products, except for the consumption of their own mothers' milk. There are also many strictly vegetarian communities (with or without a small consumption of milk) throughout the Hindu and Buddhist world, to say nothing of small Christian communities who voluntarily abstain from meat as a religious exercise. None of these communities have shown the general breakdown of health which would have been predicted from the former physiological teachings. The Trappists, the most austere of the monastic communities, abstain altogether from meat, but sometimes consume small quantities of eggs or milk. There does exist in Western Europe a small group, the Vegans, who on religious grounds abstain completely from all animal foods, not only from meat and fish, but also from dairy products, eggs, even honey. Members of this community have been quite willing to submit to medical examination. It appears that in this case they have gone too far. The best medical opinion based on these examinations is that the human body does not really need any intake at all of animal protein as such. What is essential, however, is Vitamin B.12, which is found side by side with the animal proteins in meat and milk. Here again, however, the situation is complicated by the fact that some people appear to have intestinal microorganisms (the right bugs in their guts, as the doctors describe it in their own abbreviated language) capable of synthesising Vitamin B.12 from vegetarian sources, while others do not. In some, but by no means all cases therefore, lack of Vitamin B.12 can lead to very serious consequences.[11]

In any case, a very small quantity of meat, fish, eggs or milk—and the strictest Hindu or Buddhist

[11] I am indebted to Dr Hugh Sinclair, Magdalen College, Oxford, for this information.

would be able to take at any rate one of these—will suffice, provided that good-quality vegetable protein is consumed. But to describe quality with any degree of precision is still beyond us. Subject to this qualification, it is clear that any community living predominantly on grain, at rates up to half to two-thirds of a kilogram (500–667 grams) per day, even if they only contain the minimum of 8 per cent protein, will abundantly satisfy their protein requirements.

While grains contain comparatively abundant protein, sugars and fats contain none, and the root crops—potatoes, yams, tapioca, etc.—very little. It is among people consuming substantial quantities of root crops in their diet that protein deficiencies are likely to appear. And obviously it is the children who are likely to suffer most.

A very serious medical condition, known in Africa as *kwashiorkor*, the consequence of protein deficiency in children (and sometimes in adults), is found in a number of areas of Africa and Asia. It can be rapidly reversed by an adequate protein diet. That favoured in Africa contains 10 per cent fish meal or 18 per cent dried milk. For treatment of these known deficiency diseases, however, Scrimshaw found in Guatemala that a preparation of high-quality vegetable protein (known as *incaparina*) would suffice, without animal protein.[12]

Some biochemists have also indicated that proteins derived from leaves tend to be superior to those derived from grains and seeds. It is hardly physically

[12] I am indebted to Professor Brock, Cape Town, and Professor Waterlow, University of the West Indies, for the above information.

possible to obtain the major part of one's protein by eating green vegetables, but one should do one's best. Fresh green vegetables and salads, and milk, are also important sources of most of the vitamins and minerals which the body requires. There follows the important conclusion that the only people likely to suffer from vitamin and mineral deficiency (whose consequences can again be very serious) are those living on industrially processed and stored foods. Simple agricultural and nomadic peoples may sometimes be gravely short of calories and proteins; but the minor items which they include in their diets will almost certainly safeguard them from any vitamin or mineral shortage.

We are still a long way from being able to estimate, with any real precision, how many people in the world are hungry, in the sense of lack of calories, or suffering from protein shortage. The first gap in our knowledge is our inability to estimate the total food supplies for some large countries, such as China or Indonesia. But even when we are able to ascertain them, we will then again be faced with the problem of ascertaining how evenly or unevenly they are distributed between families. In India, for instance, a food supply which, averaged over the whole population, is adequate, though without much margin to spare, is still distributed very unevenly between families. The caste system has been formally abolished by legislation, but still prevails in fact, and is likely to do so for many decades in the future. An Indian medical study of a village in Mysore brings this out clearly.

The fishermen, who are a separate hereditary caste,

are certainly underfed. The next two castes have enough to eat, with a small margin, but may be short of protein. The higher castes consume considerably more than the village average. The differences in body weight are slight, and represent the amount of flesh on the bones rather than differences in body structure. These castes have been living at these different levels of diet probably for many centuries. There is little support for the idea that the differences in body weight among the races of the world are to be explained by prolonged exposure to different diets.

Food consumption and body weights of different castes in an individual Indian village

	Average income Rs./person/month	Food consumption calories/person/day	Average body weights of adults kg. Male	Female
Fishermen	6½	1580	48	41
Harijans (low caste)	7½	1940	46	40
Miscellaneous castes	10	1960	48	41
Agricultural castes	8	2440	49	41
Brahmins and Vaisyas	18	2720	51	45

Source: Swaminathan and others, *Indian Journal of Medical Research*, November 1960.

But even after we have explained, so far as we can, the unequal distribution of food between families, we are left with a further problem about which we know very little indeed, namely the unequal distribution of food within the family. The high-protein foods are, after all, the more palatable; and in many communities where protein supplies are scanty, there is always a possibility that fathers of families will consume more than their fair share, not so much out of greed as from simple lack of knowledge that such proteins are urgently needed by growing children.

If the calorie and protein contents of the different grains are much the same, why do they suffer so much in esteem, and in economic value? Why are people willing to pay so much more for white bread? Why these jokes about Scotsmen and oats?

To some extent it is simply a matter of taste, and *de gustibus non disputandum*. Asians who live largely on a rice diet not only strongly dislike the idea of eating any other grain, but distinguish carefully between a great number of different varieties of rice, and can even detect and appreciate the improved flavour which occurs when it has been stored for a time. Our historical sociologists tell us how white bread became a social symbol throughout Europe.

But apart from these questions of taste, the coarser grains, particularly barley and maize—poor people's grains which are always sold much more cheaply per calorie unit than wheat or rice—do suffer from the real objection that they have a much higher fibre content. This not only affects their flavour, but makes them less digestible, and liable to promote flatulence.

In the field of protein requirements, it is now clearly established that some of the amino-acids which may be critically short in certain diets can be synthesised in the laboratory. It is not yet clear, however, how much it would cost, and whether it would be economically and administratively possible to distribute large quantities of laboratory preparations to, say, primitive maize-eating tribes in Africa. Attempts to go further, and to polymerise mixtures of amino-acid derivatives, in order to create what might be called whole artificial proteins, are suspected by bio-chemists as liable to lead to compounds with undesirable biological properties.

2

The Provision of Food

THE GROWTH of plants depends primarily on the strange process of photosynthesis, whereby they take energy from the sunlight and the gas carbon dioxide from the atmosphere to build up edible carbohydrates and proteins, the whole process turning on the complex molecule of chlorophyll. Plants require water to take part in their own internal chemical processes, and also for the important purpose of keeping themselves cool in warm weather. The plant relies on its roots to draw from the soil not only water, but also a number of chemical elements. Like ourselves, every plant requires a great variety of elements in minute quantities, or trace-elements; and in different parts of the world there have been astonishing experiments showing how yields of crops and grass have been very greatly increased by spraying the soil with minute quantities of such unexpected chemical elements as copper, manganese, boron and molybdenum.

But apart from these trace-elements, the plant's roots have to draw from the soil substantial quantities of nitrogen, phosphorus, potassium, calcium, sulphur, magnesium, iron and silicon. The four latter appear to be present in adequate quantities in almost every soil. Plant growth, however, may be affected by inadequate supplies of any of the first four.

Some sensitive readers may have been disturbed by the recurrence of the word "chemical". Chemicals, they say, are something which you produce in a laboratory or chemical works, and the life-processes of plants are something quite different. They are mistaken. It is quite true that some crucially important life-processes in a plant are of such complexity that we cannot imitate them in the laboratory and perhaps never will be able to do so. But there are other elements in the plant's life-processes where chemical compounds, and chemical reactions, can be clearly identified; and these are found to be exactly the same as the chemicals and reactions which we handle in

CHLOROPHYLL A

From 'Biological Chemistry' by H. R. Mahler & E. H. Cordes

the laboratory. Those who object to chemical fertiliser should know that the chemical elements and radicles which plants are observed to take up from the soil are precisely the same as those supplied by the chemical fertilisers. It is true that there may be certain circumstances under which the application of chemical fertilisers is unnecessary or even harmful, and there are other circumstances where the application of more organic manure is desirable (just as there are also some circumstances in which soils find themselves burdened with an excess of organic matter). But it is quite impermissible to elevate conclusions drawn from any of these occasional special circumstances into a general principle.

Farmyard manure and other organic fertilisers consist of plant residues, principally straw, and animal excreta and residues. The addition of substantial quantities of organic matter to soils has the principal effect of altering the structure and raising the water-holding capacity of the soil, and is therefore highly beneficial when dealing with light soils in climates liable to moisture-deficiency. There is little if any need for such additions to heavy clay soils. Moorland soils and kindred soils in high, cold country, on the other hand, nearly always contain excessive moisture and excessive organic matter, and benefit from anything which can be done to reduce them.

The real reason for the preoccupation with farmyard manure, which preoccupation has now largely disappeared among farmers, though it is still held by some of their critics, arises from the fact that until about a century ago it was the only available manure, was always scarce, and had to be husbanded carefully.

Apart from its content of bulky organic matter (which could also be supplied by ploughing in stubbles, and sometimes even by growing a green crop for the purpose of ploughing in), farmyard manure, in those days, was also the only source of the really scarce and valuable chemical elements required in the soil, nitrogen, phosphorus and potassium. (Calcium could be provided, then as now, by liming or marling.)

Four-fifths of all the air which we breathe consists of nitrogen. Each man passes literally tons of plain nitrogen through his lungs each year without getting any value from it whatever, except to dilute the oxygen which is necessary to maintain life, but which would be very bad for us in undiluted form. At the same time, nitrogen plays an absolutely critical role in keeping us fed, being the basis of all the proteins. Animal proteins can only come from animals who have consumed proteins from plants, and who may in fact waste up to four-fifths of their nitrogen intake in the process of converting plant protein to animal. Plants form their protein from nitrogen which they have taken up from the soil by means of their roots, in the form of simple chemical radicles, of which the soil may or may not yield an adequate supply, but which can now be readily supplemented by chemical fertilisers. In the absence of chemical fertilisers, however, the growth of plants is entirely dependent on the "nitrogen cycle", principally the return of nitrogen to the soil in plant and animal refuse. An important exception to this rule, however, has been provided by the leguminous plants, of which beans and peas, vetches and clover are the best-known examples.

These plants harbour, in nodules on their roots, certain micro-organisms which possess the valuable property of being able to extract nitrogen from the atmosphere and feed it into the plant's roots. In addition, it has recently been discovered that blue-green algae, which are present in certain soils, particularly swampy soils, also possess this property of being able to extract nitrogen directly from the air. It has been known for some time that certain soil micro-organisms also possess this capacity, but the amount of nitrogen which they can fix in the soil has been shown to be limited. Furthermore, a limited amount of atmospheric nitrogen is fixed, and brought down to the earth in the form of nitrates by thunderstorms. Nitrogen-bearing chemical fertilisers are now almost without exception prepared by various processes for fixing nitrogen out of the atmosphere, the first of which was discovered in 1905.

Without chemical fertilisation, however, the nitrogen content of some soils can be very low, particularly in tropical climates. The output from the soil, in its successive stages of plants, livestock and human food, returns most of its nitrogen to the soil in the form of litter and excreta; some escapes to the atmosphere in the form of ammonia, or is decomposed right back to the original inactive atmospheric nitrogen, particularly when grass or other products are burned.

Phosphorus and potassium, on the other hand, also essential for plant growth, though not in such large quantities as nitrogen, have no large reservoir in the atmosphere on which they can ultimately draw. In this case we are entirely dependent on re-cycling. As mineral elements, unlike nitrogen, they survive burning, and the ashes of grass, straw, etc., return phosphorus and potassium fully to the soil. The cycle can be altered favourably when we bring in chemical fertilisers, though in this case, unlike nitrogen, we are not using the limitless atmosphere as our basic material, but the limited deposits of raw phosphate and potassium salts found in various parts of the world. The cycle can be affected unfavourably when one region persistently sends large quantities of food to be consumed elsewhere; or when, as in modern industrial communities, the sewage is discharged, directly or indirectly, into the sea, rather than being restored to the land. Though it is not an immediate prospect, at some future date our descendants may find themselves faced with the task of extracting phosphorus and potassium from the sea for the purpose of re-cycling. They are of course present in the sea, but only in small quantities, and extraction may prove costly.

Now, however, let us go back to the beginning, to the simplest forms of food production. Sooner or later, every discussion on food supplies brings one to the question of algae. These are microscopic plants growing in water, each consisting of a single cell. Under certain circumstances they may multiply rapidly, as when they produce a disagreeable-looking scum on the surface of ornamental ponds. There is an interesting but unconfirmed legend that the ancient Aztecs used to collect and eat algae from lake surfaces. But as food they appear to have considerable drawbacks. Even though they contain protein they do not appear attractive as human food. They have very tough cell walls, and even fish find that they cannot digest them raw. Considerable processing would be required to extract edible carbohydrates or protein from them.

More encouraging are the processes, developed by Dr Pirie at Rothamsted, for extracting edible and nutritious protein from leaves of the kind which we cannot normally eat, even when cooked, because of their high fibre content—grass in particular. Grass protein, though nutritious, is completely tasteless. Visitors to Dr Pirie's laboratory are given it in their sandwiches, covered up by other flavours, and informed afterwards. The process still appears to be fairly costly. At some date in the future, however, it may be developed on a substantial scale.

Another possible source of protein, of course, is the ocean. The numbers of fish which we eat are trivial compared with the numbers which the ocean breeds. The Southern Ocean, where very few people ever go, breeds huge quantities of microscopic plankton, high in protein. It is paradoxical that the largest animal should be dependent on the smallest food source; some species of whale keep themselves fed by permanently browsing through these seas of plankton, filtering it between their finely-set teeth. Here again, however, the cost of fishing for plankton has been found to be high in relation to the present-day cost of alternative protein sources.

Yeasts are another possible source of protein. They can be provided with nitrogen in a cheap form as chemical fertilisers. Experiments so far have not been very encouraging about the ability of yeast to produce a palatable human food, or an animal food at economic cost.

Some quite encouraging experiments are now in progress, however, with micro-organisms which live —believe it or not—on oil-refinery residues and chemically-supplied nitrogen to produce a useful protein.

Still more ambitious are projects to imitate the chemical processes whereby the nodules on the roots of leguminous plants extract nitrogen from the air, at a very much lower expenditure of energy than in our industrial plants producing synthetic nitrogenous fertilisers.

That ashes of vegetation provide valuable fertiliser as far as phosphorus and potassium are concerned (and also calcium), though not nitrogen, has been understood, more or less, by primitive cultivators. The simplest form of agriculture, practised in some parts of Europe until quite recently, and still the general practice in most of Africa and in some regions of Asia and Latin America, where land is comparatively abundant, is to cut down and burn a patch of forest or scrub, thereby both fertilising the ground and clearing it of all weeds, though leaving it somewhat deficient in organic matter and nitrogen, and then to plant seeds in the ashes. In the course of years of growth, the deep roots of trees have brought up from the subsoil and leave in the ashes comparatively abundant supplies of the mineral elements. However, the soil fertility obtained by this method soon falls off. The cultivation is then abandoned, and a fresh patch of scrub or forest cleared.

But we have not yet gone right back to the beginning. The whole of the human race, for the greater part of the long time that we have been on this earth, lived almost entirely by hunting and fishing, as do a few remote tribes to this day, such as the Hottentots and Pygmies in Africa—small quantities of naturally-occurring seeds and roots are also included in their diet. Almost entirely meat-eating are the Australian aborigines who live out of contact with the whites, and the Eskimos are entirely meat and fish eaters—no edible plants grow in their climate.

To live entirely on meat in this manner could be described as being, in a sense, biologically wasteful. Such people have to consume valuable protein food merely in order to provide their calorie requirements. The weight of meat which they need to eat per day is about equal to the weight of grain which a grain-consuming people have to eat. Anthropologists and archaeologists report that a tribe living by primitive hunting and fishing has difficulty in supporting itself unless it has undisputed right over hunting grounds to the extent of about 10 km² per person[1] even in fairly good climates, and needing much more land in arid or cold climates.

However, it appears that these primitive hunters organise their affairs very badly. Scientists and pastoralists are beginning to pay attention to the question of the stock of game which such semi-arid land can carry.[2] Minimum meat requirements may be put at 200 kg. (one-fifth of a ton) per person per year. For each pound of beef that we eat (averaging all cuts together) we need 1·8 pounds of liveweight ox; and we throw away, or convert into fertiliser or soap or

[1] i.e. about 4 sq. miles (2·59 km² = 1 sq. mile).
[2] For some interesting results, see Pirie, *Journal of the Royal Statistical Society*, April 1962.

dog biscuits or pig meal, many parts of the carcase which the primitive man would be willing to eat, especially if he is complaining about being hungry. His annual requirements, measured liveweight, should therefore be about one-third of a ton. How much stock will be required to give this yield of game depends on whether it consists of small animals reproducing themselves rapidly, or large animals reproducing themselves slowly. If we make the very cautious assumption that the stock of game reproduces its own weight only every three years, then a stock of game weighing one ton liveweight would suffice to produce the third of a ton liveweight needed to keep one primitive man in meat. But the available information for Africa shows that 10 km² of indigenous bushland will carry a stock of anything from 50 to 150 tons of game. (This latter figure is very much higher than the estimates of the quantity of cattle which can be pastured on the same area of land, which range from 4 to 28 tons liveweight—the indigenous animals are much better adapted to do well on the grazing available, and are also more resistant to disease and parasites.)

Really then, how does primitive man manage to make such difficulties about keeping himself fed on land which carries anywhere from 50 to 150 times the amount of game which he appears to require? There are two reasons for this. The first is that he does not have the land to himself, but has to share it with carnivorous animals. They are everywhere—the great felines in the tropics, wolves in the north, dingoes in Australia, polar bears in the Arctic. It is they who eat the bulk of the game; and until man is both numerous enough and skilful enough to extirpate them, they will continue to do so.

The second reason is that when primitive hunters do succeed in killing a large animal, they have no means of preserving it (except the Eskimos, who have natural refrigeration provided). They do their best to preserve it internally, by eating as fast as they can when the meat is available. Among the Siriono hunting tribe in South America, a group of four men has been seen to consume a peccary weighing 27 kg. at a single sitting. The African bushmen, who live in a very arid and difficult climate, and will even eat a leopard if they can catch him, have the interesting physiological adaptation of highly elastic stomachs, and ability to store large quantities of nutriment in the form of additional body fat, which they lay on in a good season and keep as a reserve.

To take another example, some of the coldest mountain land in the North of Scotland, with a near-Arctic climate, nevertheless produces venison at a rate which would feed one person on 6 km². Again, however, this is on the assumption that it is all available for human consumption, and does not have to be shared with the wolves—in fact the Scots did not succeed in finally extirpating their wolves until the end of the eighteenth century.

When men do become more numerous and better organised, and can extirpate or at any rate keep in check the carnivores, they may then cease to live by hunting and either become owners of tame animals, or agriculturists.

Nomadic grazing and agriculture in fact represented two alternative lines of development (Cain and

Stages of Development of Agriculture and Stockbreeding

I Pre-agricultural Man (living by hunting, fishing, gathering
wild fruits and roots)

Pre-lithic tools
Palaeolithic tools

IIA Agricultural Man   IIB Nomadic
Pastoral Man

Shifting cultivation   Neolithic tools

Settled cultivation

Bronze tools
Iron tools

Abel in the Book of Genesis; and agriculture got a black mark). Nomadic grazing communities may have preceded agriculture, which began, so far as we know, about 7000 B.C. in the Middle East. The early agricultural communities (and indeed the present-day shifting cultivators), though they could not exactly be described as nomadic, were not settled, and might shift their cultivation over fairly wide areas. By gradual stages the pastoral communities became agricultural, in many cases in the mixed economy which practised both cultivation and stockbreeding. But some communities living entirely on nomadic grazing persist to this day in Central Asia and in some parts of Africa. However, even in these cases, they no longer live solely on meat and milk. They have trading relations with neighbouring agricultural peoples, and buy cereal foods from them in exchange for some of their livestock products.

Now let us look more closely at the shifting cultivators. The two principal features of their agricultural life are something which we find difficult to grasp, living as we do in a cool rainy climate, with mechanised agriculture. Most of the shifting cultivators live in a monsoonal climate, in which the rainfall is confined almost entirely to a few months in the year, the rest of the year being very hot and dry. Food for the whole year therefore has to be grown in the short rainy season. The food plants grow very fast—but so do the weeds.

The other thing we have to remember is that their crops have to be grown entirely by hand cultivation. Tractors are of course out of the question; but so, for most of them, are draught horses or oxen. In many parts of Africa draught animals are killed off by tsetse-fly infestation. But even if they were not, the tribesmen would be too poor to maintain them. There is little grazing in the dry season, and the draught animals would compete with the human population for the limited supply of cultivated foodstuffs. The principal problem of the shifting cultivator is the rapid loss of the fertility of his soil. When growing maize or similar cereal crops, he finds that the land is no longer worth cultivating when the yield falls to about 600 kg. per hectare.[3] On the average-sized plot cultivated, this is still a long way above the minimum required to feed himself and his dependants; but it is at this point that he decides that further cultivation of land is not worth the effort, and that it is better to clear a fresh site.

The number of years of cultivation before the yield

[3] 1 hectare = 2·47 acres. 600 kg./hectare = 675 lb./acre. This represents only one-seventh of the present average yield in the USA.

falls to this minimum varies very much with the soil. On what are described by Allen[4] as "strong red earths and clays" cultivation may be maintained for as long as 14 years. But these are unusual. On "transitional" soils cultivation is abandoned on the average after seven years. On the "plateau or sandveld" soils, which constitute so much of the area of Africa, cultivation has to be abandoned after four years on good soils, two years on mediocre soils, and the poorer soils cannot be cultivated at all.

The time required for the bush to regenerate sufficiently to yield another round of fertile soil after clearing and burning is estimated at 15 years at a minimum, and 20 years is generally considered preferable.

The maximum amount of land which can be cultivated under these conditions is about 0·8 hectare per member of the tribe, i.e. about 1·6 hectares per able-bodied worker. Men and women both work all out during the short rainy season; about half the tribe will consist of children and non-able-bodied adults. It is only when conditions are bad, however, that the tribe will cultivate this maximum area, which under normal conditions should yield them a good deal more than the minimum required for subsistence. Most tribes, apart from those living in the remotest areas, want to produce a certain amount of grain or other produce for sale, in addition to their subsistence requirements. If we assume 0·8 hectare cultivated per person, and 20 years' cycle between cultivations, two years' cultivation in each cycle, and a third of the land uncultivable, we can agree with the figure often

[4] *The African Husbandman.*

stated by African experts of 8 persons per km^2 as the maximum population density which can be supported by this type of agriculture.

It is worth mentioning that it is not until population density has risen to about 27 persons per km^2 that it is possible to drive away the wild animals and to cut the scrub sufficiently to keep the tsetse fly in check. Only a settled agricultural population, and not a shifting population, can attain this density.

It is tempting to theorise that shifting cultivation is the earliest form of agriculture, and that the arts of intensive agriculture are learned later. But the distinguished French geographer Gourou has adduced considerable evidence to show that the shifting cultivators who still occupy most of Africa have the knowledge of intensive agriculture, but prefer not to practise it because it calls for greater effort on their part, which they will not exert while land is abundant. In a few places in Africa, tribes which have been isolated by their enemies in remote locations without any opportunity of practising shifting agriculture—including one interesting example of a tribe living on the small island of Ukara in Lake Victoria—have practised extremely intensive agriculture, with high yields.

It was Gourou also who developed some interesting speculations about the fate of the Maya civilisation. It was only discovered comparatively recently that what is now almost unpopulated thick jungle country in Southern Mexico and Guatemala was once the home of a civilisation probably more advanced than that of the Aztecs and the Incas, building fine stone cities, and showing evidence of considerable knowledge of astronomy and mathematics. This civilisation disappeared completely about the sixth century A.D. Gourou suggested that the reason for the disappearance of the Maya civilisation, while the Inca and Aztec civilisations survived, was that, while the two latter depended on settled intensive agriculture with artificial watering, the Maya civilisation attempted to feed itself from shifting agriculture, working on a cycle of only 4 to 5 years.[5] Under these circumstances, the soil near to the cities would soon have become exhausted, and the Maya would have been compelled to cultivate land progressively further afield, until difficulties of transport (all three of these ancient American civilisations depended solely upon human porterage) caused their civilisation to disintegrate. (The Incas avoided this fate by cultivating fertile desert soils by means of irrigation: the Aztecs by drawing supplies from a wider area by means of boat transport on a lake.)

Gourou considers that repeated cutting and burning of thick tropical forest leads to re-growth of increasing sparsity, until it is eventually replaced by a thin "savannah" type of tree cover, which yields much less stored fertility. There is little doubt that this is true. In general, climate determines the boundary between tropical rain forest and savannah, but only in a broad manner, and the precise demarcation depends very much on the quality of the soil.

Some people would have it that the clearing of tropical forests reduces the rainfall. Meteorologists will not, however, concede a millimetre of this. Rainfall, they say, depends on what is happening in the

[5] *See also* Morley, *The Ancient Maya*, Oxford, 1946.

atmosphere, and no amount of cutting of trees, planting of them, establishing artificial lakes, etc., makes the slightest difference. What may happen, however, is a very considerable deterioration of the soil[6]; and these changes in the soil may give people the impression that the rainfall has changed.

The clearing and burning itself does little damage to the soil. The main harm, from the cultivator's point of view, comes from the spread of weeds, which he has difficulty in keeping down with his hand-tools. In the high-rainfall tropics, the weeds grow faster, but there is less danger of permanent infestation. More trouble arises in monsoonal areas, i.e. those with a short rainy season and a long dry spell, under which circumstances deep-rooted grasses can get a hold, and not be choked out by subsequent growth.

Another serious trouble is soil erosion. This is primarily, of course, a question of slope. Flat land is by its nature immune from water erosion, though it may suffer some loss of soil through wind erosion under exceptional circumstances. In agriculture on established farm land in temperate climates we are accustomed to seeing quite steep slopes being cultivated. But the following consideration should be borne in mind. In the temperate regions most of the rain comes in showers of light or moderate intensity, not in the sudden heavy downpours which characterise tropical and sub-tropical climates. Secondly, when the soil is already fairly moist, it is much less likely to be washed away than is a soil whose surface has been thoroughly dried by a hot sun. Finally, the

[6] Nye and Greenland, *The Soil under Shifting Cultivation*, Commonwealth Agricultural Bureau.

presence of abundant organic matter in the soil aug-
ments its water-holding capacity, and also helps it to
resist erosion in storms. The United States in the
1930s suddenly (and quite rightly) became concerned about soil erosion, particularly in the Southern
States. At first scientists tended to blame individual
crops, particularly maize, sugar cane and tobacco. But
it is now apparent that any crop, grown well and
carefully with an adequate input of fertiliser, and
with stubble and litter ploughed in, will probably
leave the soil higher in organic matter than before;
while any crop grown badly will have the opposite
effect. The effects of erosion on slopes can also be
combated by the device of ploughing horizontally
along the contours, instead of ploughing up and down
the slope, when the furrows encourage erosive run-
off of water. In these ways the downward spiral of
soil erosion, which was beginning to appear in the
United States, has been reversed and replaced by a
beneficial spiral of improving soil fertility with each
succeeding crop.

But neither the scientific knowledge nor the
methods of the United States are available to the shifting cultivators of the tropics and sub-tropics. (We
must include pastoralists too; it is generally the
steeper lands that are grazed, and heavy stocking
during the dry season may leave these slopes completely bare of vegetation, and therefore extremely
subject to erosion when the rain comes.) Erosion at
first appears in the form of some of the topsoil being
removed and carried away as silt in the streams. If
extensive, erosion leads to a loss of soil fertility. In
its worst form gullies appear in the soil, gradually

increasing in size, until it becomes impossible to cultivate the land.

Erosion is likely to be most acute in the high-rainfall tropical forest areas. In the low-rainfall country it is not likely to be a problem. Here the soil is only sparsely covered with vegetation, and has been grazed nearly bare each year for millions of dry seasons by the native animals. Under these circumstances all possible erosion has already taken place. Over these very long periods of time, most of the steep slopes have already been washed away, except of course where they take the form of rock faces, which the rain cannot affect. In the high-rainfall tropics on the other hand, numerous moderate and steep slopes are found, protected from erosion by the thick growth of vegetation. When this land is cleared, unless strong measures are taken to maintain the organic content of the soil, erosion is likely to be rapid.

In "Black Africa"—that is to say, Africa south of the Sahara, and north of South Africa—only 3 per cent of the available land, so Gourou estimates, is actually cultivated in any one year. Peoples possessed of land in such abundance can afford to practise shifting agriculture. We have seen, however, that when the local pressure of population is increased, for one reason or another, they are then compelled to give up shifting cultivation and to practise settled agriculture, which represents a much more productive use of the land, but at the same time requires them to work harder—which of course is the principal reason why they do not adopt it until they have to.

A number of situations, both in history and in the present-day world, have been analysed in an interesting book[7] by the Danish economist Ester Boserup. It will be seen that this is an exact reversal of the Malthusian theory of population. The Rev. Thomas Robert Malthus published in 1798 his book entitled *The Principles of Population*, which has had a very wide influence, though most of those who now call themselves Malthusians advocate proposals very different from those which Malthus supported.

Malthus thought that the whole history of the world indicated populations growing rapidly until they reached "the limit of subsistence", after which their numbers were forcibly held down by "vice and misery", unless they adopted what to him seemed the rational solution, namely deferment of marriage. Of any other form of restriction of conception he strongly disapproved; modern methods of contraception were of course unknown in his time, but in the 1817 edition of his book, he had some curious prevision of them, and foresaw striking consequences: "If it were possible for each married couple to limit by a wish the number of their children, there is certainly reason to fear that the indolence of the human race would be very greatly increased; and that neither the population of individual countries, nor of the whole earth, would ever reach the proper and natural extent."

This interesting statement represented a profound modification of Malthus's earlier position, admitting that the world might not be everywhere peopled so nearly up to the limit of subsistence as he had previously supposed. However "Malthusians" have continued for nearly two centuries to go on expounding

[7] *The Conditions of Agricultural Growth.*

the cruder theory, that while improvements in agricultural productivity may come, their consequence is always an increase in population, which brings the human race back as near to the edge of famine as before. We can now see that the "Malthusians" have got things upside down. It is not an improvement in agricultural productivity which promotes population growth. It is population growth which promotes improvements in agricultural (and industrial) productivity. And the reason why things happen this way and not the other way round is the same as in the case of the transition from shifting cultivation to settled agriculture in Africa—namely that the new and more productive methods, at any rate when first adopted, call for harder work and changes in settled habits.

When a tribe which has hitherto lived by hunting begins cultivation, cutting and burning mature forest growth, they obtain a soil which a gardener would greatly appreciate, loose and friable, and covered with fertilising ash. Seeds can be planted in this soil with a simple digging stick. It is after repeated burning of the re-growth, however, that "forest fallow" gives place to the less productive "bush fallow". Not only do a certain number of weed and grass roots survive fires. The soil is becoming more compact, and has to be cultivated laboriously with hand-hoes, instead of simply planting seeds with a digging stick. The weeding routine also becomes more arduous, and indeed sets a narrow limit to the amount of land which each cultivator can tend. In the final stage the land becomes full of perennial grass roots, which cannot be killed by hand-hoeing. A substantial plough, drawn by draught animals, is the only means by which such land can now be kept in cultivation.

Boserup is of the opinion that nomadic pastoral tribes are by no means necessarily the first and simplest form of agricultural organisation. In many cases they may represent, as it were, an economic degeneration, or any rate a side-line, of a people that had cultivated their land to this limit, and then were for some reason unable or unwilling to start settled cultivation with draught animals. So they took to nomadic herding instead.

There is no doubt that, when it first begins, settled agriculture with draught animals appears laborious and distasteful to people who hitherto practised shifting agriculture, under which they only had to work for a few months a year—just as even the simplest forms of shifting agriculture appeared very laborious to people who had hitherto enjoyed a simple life of hunting and fishing. Draught animals have to be watched and tended throughout the year. Pasture is not always available, and they sometimes have to consume a share of the agricultural produce.

For these settled agricultural communities, before the advent of chemical fertilisers, the problem of maintaining soil fertility was of course acute, however carefully they husbanded animal manure, village refuse, used thatch, pond mud and the like. They generally found it necessary to fallow the land for alternate years, i.e. keep it cultivated to destroy weeds, and to enable it to recover some fertility. About the ninth century A.D. our ancestors in Northern Europe, finding that population was increasing again after long centuries of chaos and disaster, were forced in consequence to adopt an important innovation which economised land, namely the three-course rotation (wheat, barley, fallow). As well as economising land, this new agricultural system made possible an intricate and ingenious reorganisation of working methods which provided for a better distribution over the year of man and ox labour.

Our ideas about further improvements in agricultural methods tend to be rather limited and insular. We have all read in our history books about the so-called "Agricultural Revolution" of the eighteenth century, in which a number of legendary figures with names like "Turnip" Townshend discovered how to grow root crops, keep cattle alive through the winter, and organise a four-course rotation. Like so many history-book statements, this is a half-truth—but with the most important half left out. Turnips for cattle feeding, so far from being a discovery of eighteenth-century England, were mentioned in Virgil's *Georgics*, and in agricultural textbooks of the ancient world. Knowledge of root crops, of lucerne, and of many other ways of obtaining more agricultural produce from a limited amount of land, was available but remained unused until increasing population demanded it. In the most densely populated parts of medieval Europe, Northern Italy and the Low Countries, these improvements were appearing many centuries before the English so-called "Agricultural Revolution". English farmers in fact obtained many ideas, and much technical help, from the Low Countries.

In Asia there are many areas of high-rainfall land

very densely populated, including Taiwan, Java, East Pakistan, Bengal and Kerala in India. One of the best technical methods of improving their agricultural output is by double-cropping, already extensively practised in Taiwan. This, however, will call for drastic changes in many long-established customs. Crops and grazing will have to be properly fenced, and livestock tethered, instead of being free to graze at will over all the village stubbles once the harvest has been gathered. These grazing rights, however, are among the most valuable possessions of the poorest families, who will try to defend them to the last. The situation bears an unhappy resemblance to the English enclosures of the sixteenth to eighteenth centuries, which were necessary for the improvement of agricultural efficiency, though carried out with grave social injustice. Efficiency and justice can be combined; but although we have had the benefit of this long experience, we have not yet told the world how it can be done.

Fortunately, for modern Asia, there is a quicker and more remunerative method of improving agricultural output, to be applied even before it becomes necessary to undertake the difficult task of organising double-cropping, namely greatly increased application of chemical fertilisers. How large are the returns to be obtained from them we shall see shortly.

3

The Stages of Agricultural Development

IN CHAPTER 1 we estimated the amount of grain which is required to provide the absolute minimum of calories and proteins, assuming that requirements of vitamins (including the essential vitamin B.12), minerals, and so on, could be obtained from a few salad vegetables, frogs, snails, etc. But "Man shall not live by bread alone", even in the physical sense. There must be some relief from extreme monotony of the diet, and some more definite provision for green vegetables, and for a minimum of animal protein. Another factor which we tend to forget is that poor communities do not make their clothes out of nylon. They require, at the very minimum, about $1\frac{1}{2}$ kg. per person per year of cotton, flax, wool or other fibre to make their clothes. These also are agricultural products.

We are now confronted with the necessity of devising a single unit in which disparate forms of agricultural production can be measured. For poor communities, in which grain, of necessity, constitutes the principal agricultural product, one kilogram of grain-equivalent represents a convenient unit in which to measure the comparatively small output of vegetables, fibres, meat, etc. Conversion to grain-equivalent units is *not* in terms of calories. If we calculated in this way, we would undervalue the valuable proteins in meat, and give no value at all to fibres. These other products are therefore converted to grain-equivalents by their *economic* values, that is to say, the number of kilograms of grain for which 1 kilogram of the product in question exchanges in the local markets.

This useful device of grain-equivalents was

developed in China in the 1930s by J. L. Buck, an American agricultural economist who was able to make a thorough survey of Chinese agriculture during a brief interval in which the country was comparatively free from disturbances. It was used as a general measure of comparative agricultural progress throughout Asia by De Vries, a Dutch economist who had long worked in Indonesia. It was De Vries who first showed that these units of grain-equivalents per head of population (including non-agricultural population) served as a general measure of agricultural progress.

Agricultural and Livestock Production

Expressed in grain-equivalents, kg./person/year

Under 300	Subsistence hand-tool agriculture or grazing
300–500	Subsistence hand-tool agriculture or grazing with some trade
500–750	Agriculture with draught animals and grazing herds
Over 750	Mixed farming including the feeding of grains and concentrates to pigs, poultry and other animals

Bearing in mind what has been said above about the need for supplementary foods, textile fibres, etc., and to provide a small allowance for wastage, we can say in round figures that any community whose food supply is 250 kg. grain-equivalent per person per year is living at the real subsistence level. (The word "subsistence" is often loosely and emotively used to describe any income considered low; it is as well to reserve the word for its precise medical meaning.) Any community producing at a rate between 250 and

300 kg. might well be expected to consume any further food or fibre which they produced.

Even beyond 300 kg., the standard of feeding is still vastly lower than anything to which we are accustomed. But it is fallacious to conclude that it must necessarily follow that any further food produced beyond this limit will also be consumed. Of course the people concerned would like to eat better. But agricultural and nutritional enthusiasts forget that people have other needs too. They urgently want better clothing, building materials to improve their houses, medicines, perhaps school books for their children. When the level of productivity has gone a little above the figure of 300 units, part of the additional output will not be consumed, but will be traded for the purpose of buying these other urgently-needed goods.

At these low levels of productivity the agricultural work will all be done with hand-tools. An important turning-point is reached at about 500 units. At this level it becomes possible to maintain draught animals. While they have to consume part of the agricultural output (except in a few areas where grazing is unusually abundant) they nevertheless can also add to it considerably, and represent an important upward step in the path of progress.

West Pakistan and most of India, apart from a few high-rainfall areas, however, constitute an exception which "proves" this rule. Though their productivity is below 500 units, they nevertheless employ draught animals. In their case it is a climatic necessity. The monsoon season is so short that they could not possibly get all the cultivation done by hand, however hard they worked. However, these draught animals, which have to be fed well in the season when they are expected to work, constitute a very serious demand on a limited food supply, and their owners often go hungry. In India the problem is greatly accentuated by the religious prohibition upon the slaughter of uneconomic cattle.

An important element in our diet is provided by pigs and poultry, which bring us various animal protein foods in palatable and convenient form. It is a serious mistake, however, to tell the Asian and African countries that they ought to do the same. In the first place, these animals, unless kept under the carefully regulated conditions which our farmers observe, are very susceptible to diseases. But there is a more serious objection than that. Farm animals fall into two principal biological classes, the ruminants and non-ruminants. (The horse, strictly speaking, is a non-ruminant, but has an exceptional digestive system which enables him to eat grass as ruminants do.) Ruminants are able to obtain at any rate a large part of their nourishment from grass, hay and straw, which we have no wish to share with them. The non-ruminants on the other hand, among whom are the pigs and the poultry, have comparatively small and simple stomachs, as we do. They cannot digest grass and similar foods, and have to be fed on grains and root crops, for which they are direct competitors with us. Of all the calories and proteins which they consume, only a small proportion come back in meat and eggs, albeit of improved quality. A country which is doubtful about being able to provide adequate proteins for its human population certainly should not consume any of its limited supply of plant proteins in this way. It is not until productivity has reached the level of 750 kg. of grain-equivalent per person per year that the keeping of pigs and poultry becomes possible—apart from a few who live mainly on the village refuse, and make very slow growth in consequence.

After that, agricultural productivity is capable of rising continuously, without any sharp turning-points, to the high levels found in the advanced countries today.

We do not have evidence of any whole countries at or near the true subsistence level of 250 kg. per person per year, though many isolated groups are probably at or below this level from time to time. It is possible to calculate agricultural production in grain-equivalents per head for a considerable number of countries.[1] The countries producing only between 300 and 400 units in 1958 included Lebanon and Libya with 332 and 337 respectively—but these countries have substantial other sources of income, from oil and defence expenditure in Libya, and finance and industry in Lebanon, and can afford to import food. The poorest country for which we have information, which does not have other sources of income, is Guinea with an output of 351. Not far above is India with 382. Both these countries have received some food imports in the form of loans or gifts from abroad.

A number of countries are in the 400–450 units range, namely the countries constituted out of former

[1] See *The Economics of Subsistence Agriculture*, 3rd edition, pp. 72–3.

French West and Equatorial Africa, and former Belgian Congo, Tanzania, Jordan (which has other sources of income), Pakistan, South Korea, and Bolivia and Haiti in Latin America. Between 450 and 500 units are Ethiopia, Kenya, Togo and Venezuela (this latter country, however, with abundant oil income). Just above the 500 line (i.e. just capable of supporting draught animals) were Egypt, Tunisia, Angola, Liberia, Nigeria, Rhodesia, Indonesia and Guatemala.

Figures for a single year, however, can be misleading. In all these countries the weather varies considerably from year to year, and we get a clearer idea of the way things are going if we take three-year averages. This is done in the table overleaf for a number of low-productivity countries. Included also for interest are some Asian and African countries with fairly high agricultural productivity, often from export crops.

Cuba and Algeria are sad examples of a decline of formerly productive countries, due to internal political disorder; and Ceylon of very slow improvement. In Malaysia "the Emergency" is over; but it is taking some time to recover to the level of productivity of the 1930s. The decline in productivity in Iraq does not matter very much because of abundant oil revenues; or, to put it the other way round, many farmers have probably left their holdings in order to earn higher incomes in the oil-supported cities. Tunisia and Morocco are also examples of decline, though not so serious as Algeria.

Taiwan is an exceptional country. The holdings are so small that most of the country has missed De

Agricultural Production per Head of Population per Year

Kilograms of Wheat Equivalent

	1934–38	1952–54	1957–59	1964–66
Libya		323	357	474
India	357	367	382	367
Pakistan	460	455	444	441
Tunisia		430	457	390
Ethiopia		499	519	613
Indonesia	434	533	521	486
Egypt		499	534	548
Guatemala		507	540	670
Morocco		605	538	524
Honduras		534	542	555
Iran		511	586	580
Ceylon	583	568	619	655
Taiwan	775	606	642	640
Thailand	408	664	637	792
Algeria		785	672	535
Iraq		745	706	629
Philippines	515	695	708	696
Mexico		549	692	719
Syria		870	802	896
Colombia		897	861	860
Malaysia	1095	940	951	1030
Cuba		1748	1640	1339

Vries' stage of keeping draught animals, and cultivation is still done by hand, though pig-keeping is customary. Failure to recover the very high productivity of the 1930s (much of which was in the form of sugar and rice exported to Japan) has not done harm in this case, because Taiwan now has a large and rapidly growing export of manufactured goods, which will purchase imported food.

For India and Pakistan, the results since 1966 have given much more encouragement. Thailand and

Mexico are examples of very rapid advance of agricultural productivity.

For most of the world, agricultural production is advancing substantially faster than population, and is likely to continue to do so. Countries in which agricultural production has not advanced as rapidly as population over the past decade, besides those already shown in the table above, are few, and fall into the following categories.

(1) Advanced countries in which agricultural production has been deliberately limited as a matter of policy—United States, Sweden, Norway, Switzerland.

(2) Latin American countries where the growth of productivity has been checked by economic disorder—Argentina, Chile, Uruguay.

4

Food and Labour

SOME OF us get our ideas of agriculture in developing countries from recollections of the Victorian farm labourer, toiling twelve hours a day for a wage which barely sufficed to feed his family. Others have acquired the entirely different idea of an over-populated farm land divided into miserably small holdings, which provide neither adequate food nor adequate occupation to their unhappy owners, who spend most of the year resting glumly under a tree. Starting from the latter (erroneous) assumption, ingenious economists have developed theories which propose that large quantities of labour could be withdrawn from the countryside at no real cost to agriculture, and promptly put to work in industry, to the country's great benefit.

In fact, both assumptions are incorrect. It is no use economists trying to calculate the marginal productivity of agricultural labour (i.e. the supposed effect on production of withdrawing part of the labour force) in such countries, and to deduce from this how much labour could usefully be taken out of agriculture. The productivity and the requirements of labour change violently from month to month—even indeed from day to day, at some seasons of the year. Even those who never learned any geography (who seem to be regrettably numerous among the ranks of the highly-educated) should by now have acquired some idea about the nature of the monsoonal climates, in which so large a proportion of the world's population is living. Monsoonal climates are found over the greater part of the tropics and sub-tropics. Islands, and some regions near to the sea or subject to persistent prevailing maritime winds, may enjoy continuous rainfall; and some tropical areas are semi-arid or desert. The remainder receive monsoonal rainfall in accordance with a meteorological principle which can be explained in very simple terms. As the summer advances, the continental masses get heated up to a point where the accumulation of heat is sufficient to force a steady upward current of air from their surfaces. This partial vacuum necessitates an inflow of cooler and moister oceanic air, which in its turn is forced upward and compelled to discharge its moisture as rain. A most interesting fact about monsoons (of the very greatest agricultural significance) is their high degree of regularity. In many parts of India the monsoon can be counted upon to arrive about 21 June, almost to the day. The entire organisation of agriculture, and indeed of other economic and social life as well in these rural communities, depends on the timing of the monsoon. When, as occasionally happens, it fails, or comes late, the results are very serious indeed.

The duration of the monsoon varies greatly between regions. In some parts of southern India there is a short second monsoon about November. It is the monsoonal climate therefore which necessarily creates this unhappy alternation between a long dry season of enforced idleness for most people, followed by a short monsoon season when everyone has to work all hours, and farmers are conscious of an acute labour shortage. In fact, the contribution which child labour can make to the needs of the farm during this period of urgency is an important consideration among African and Asian farmers with large families. Labour requirements are spread over the year a little less unevenly where there are livestock on the farm, or diversified minor crops such as vegetables are grown. But reasonably regular employment throughout the year can only be given by a much more complex and sophisticated agriculture, such as that of Western Europe, in which livestock predominate, or of modern Japan, with a considerable output of fruit and vegetables.

In some inhabited parts of Africa the rainy season is as short as two months in each year. But the high temperatures make it possible to raise some crops, particularly millet, sorghum and groundnuts, in this short period. Here timing is absolutely all-important. In Kenya[1] sorghum, yielding 1·7 tons/hectare if planted before the rains, shows a 27 per cent reduction if planting is delayed until only *four days* after the beginning of the rains, and more than 50 per cent reduction if it is delayed for *seven days*. Maize, whose yield varies with the season from 1·5 to 2 tons/ hectare if planted before the rains, loses 40 per cent of its yield as a consequence of six days' delay. On the face of it, every prudent farmer would have the soil cultivated and sown before the rains came. But most of them find this impossible. They are faced with shortages both of labour and of oxen, and when they have the oxen they are always hungry at the end of the long dry season, and too weak to plough the hard unmoistened soil. "If farmers carried out every operation at the time indicated by agricultural officers to be necessary for optimum yields, they would in effect have to cope with a number of insur-

[1] Judith Heyer and others, quoted De Wilde, *Agricultural Development in Tropical Africa*, Vol. 2, pp. 101–2.

mountable peaks of labour demand." If a farmer does without oxen, or cannot use them during the dry season, and attempts to hand-cultivate the land, it will take him four to five months to hoe one hectare.

Even if we take planting within the first nine days after the rain as standard procedure, Heyer estimates a further 15 per cent loss in the maize or *wimbi* crop if planting is delayed to 10–15 days after the beginning of the rains, and a 35 per cent further loss after 15 days.

The cultivator has ways of meeting these problems, which call for considerable skill and ingenuity. We have a detailed study of the working timetable for the whole village in the case of Sabilpur, a densely populated village growing rice and jute in East Pakistan.[2] There is a peak demand for labour in the planting season, April-May, and harvesting and cultivation peaks in December and July. Out of 176 men and boys aged between 12 and 60 in the village, 12 (no more) were engaged in non-agricultural occupations which demanded their full-time attention, and from which they could not be diverted. The others undertook farm work and non-farm work with a certain flexibility. We can describe the situation clearly if we express the amount of work to be done in terms of average hours per week required from all the available males. Non-farm work (apart from the work of the 12 men occupied at it full-time) required about 14 hours per week from each man during most of the year. But they were able to reduce this temporarily to 8 hours in July and December and to 4

[2] M. Habibullah, *Pattern of Agricultural Unemployment*, Dacca University.

hours in the busiest part of the planting season. The total amount of work done, adding together farm work and other work, averaged 23–33 hours per man per week during the slack time of the year. These figures rose suddenly to 43 and 46 respectively in July and December (including the reduced amount of non-farm work performed). At the peak of the planting season, it was well over 50 hours. But this is not the end of the story. There was a "labour reserve" of villagers who worked for a large part of the year as labourers in the neighbouring seaport of Chittagong. This labour force was drawn on to provide, in effect, an extra two or three hours' work per head of the local labour force in the July peak, and an extra eight hours' work at the peak of the planting season. Without this reserve of labour, the planting could not be done to time, and the crops would suffer seriously.

So in this interesting arrangement for dealing with fluctuating labour requirements, the town has to provide the final reserve of labour for use in the busy season. By contrast, during the slack season, labour does not migrate to the town, but remains in the village, where it is at least partially employed. Those whose views were not reported in this study, however, are the factory and wharf employers in Chittagong, who probably heartily dislike this excessive mobility of labour. Experience from a number of developing countries shows that industrial employers strongly need experienced, reliable, permanent labour, which they are willing and able to pay much more highly than the fluctuating casual labour which they now employ.

Japan has carried this principle almost to extremes.

In wages, fringe benefits and working conditions, the regular employee of a big company is very much better off than the casual worker. Nevertheless, as the country has become more highly industrialised, part-time industrial employment is now within the reach even of members of poor farm families in remote regions. For this reason, if for no other, Japanese farmers cannot afford to leave labour idle for some months and overwork it in others. The Japanese Ministry of Agriculture in 1956 published an interesting booklet[3] illustrating what can be done even on the average minute Japanese family farm of less than 2 hectares (5 acres), with a family labour force of some 2½ adult-man-equivalents. Under the traditional pattern of single-crop rice, mulberry for feeding silk worms, and vetch as an animal food, there was an unmanageable peak labour demand of nearly 300 man-hours per week in the planting season at the beginning of June, another peak demand of 140 man-hours per week in the harvest season in October, followed by practically no demand for labour in December, January and February, and requirements of only about 50 man-hours per week in March, April and August. Careful replanning of the cropping programme to double-crop rice, to produce wheat, barley, vetch, fruit and vegetables, on small plots, and to keep poultry, kept the labour demand steadily within the range 100–150 man-hours per week throughout the year.

Let us not dismiss these questions of labour shortage and labour surplus in peasant agriculture as

[3] *Farm Planning with special reference to the Management and Improving of Small Scale Family Farming.*

minor matters affecting only those immediately concerned. They may affect the whole world. It was a misunderstanding of this problem which was the original cause of the present chaos in China.

It may seem a contradiction in terms to talk about a labour shortage in a country with the population of China. But think again. Here is this huge area to be cultivated, with virtually no tractors, and indeed hardly even any draught oxen. Much of it has to be double-cropped. To make up for the lack of fertiliser, every bit of refuse and mud has to be carefully collected, the land has to be cultivated with extreme diligence, and every weed removed. In a country so near to hunger, no wastage is permissible, and every scrap of grain has to be recovered and the straw and roots carefully hoarded for winter fuel. Under these conditions a rural population of 500–600 millions is needed just to get the work done. In the survey carried out by Buck in the 1930s, labour surplus was reported only in December and January, while two-thirds of all the villages reported that they were suffering from labour shortage in the harvest season. Chairman Mao, however, did not believe in ascertaining the accurate facts about the agriculture of his own country. He preferred his own ideas, which he made clear when he wrote his book *Socialist Upsurge*. "Under present conditions of production there would be a one-third manpower surplus in rural areas," he wrote. Then in 1958, ironically named "The Year of the Great Leap Forward", completely misled by grossly falsified statistics produced by its own officials, who believed that it was their duty to tell their superiors what they wanted to hear, the Chinese

Government announced that it had succeeded in doubling the harvest in a single year, that this gain would be permanent, that a great deal of the agricultural land could be taken out of cultivation, and that a third of the agricultural population could be transferred to such tasks as building dams by moving earth in hand baskets, and smelting steel in backyard furnaces. China spent the subsequent ten years trying to recover from the effects of this collective insanity.

Chairman Mao had received warning[4] that Chinese agriculture, even before "The Year of the Great Leap Forward", was already facing serious labour shortages. There is a mysterious Chinese proverb, which applies in the southern provinces where double-cropping of rice is practised—"In the morning yellow, in the evening green." This means that about the month of June, men have to work through the heat of the day in harvesting the first rice crop, and in the cool of the evening plant out the seedlings for the second crop. You cannot afford to have labour shortages in this type of agricultural economy.

Very different from China is Africa, where land is abundant. The primitive "cut and burn" agriculture still practised over most of Africa, while wasteful of land, is economical of labour. It does not take long to produce minimum requirements. These have been estimated, it will be remembered, at about 250 kg. (¼ ton) of grain equivalent per person. This may be

---

[4] I am indebted to Dr K. R. Walker, School of Oriental Studies, University of London, for this interesting story and quotations by Ma Yin-Chu, President of the University of Peking, one of the few independent thinkers who still survived in China in the 1950s.

expressed as about 600 kg. per cultivator, assuming that cultivators represent about half the population —women and the older children work as long as or longer than the men during the cultivating season— and allowing a small margin. Some careful measurements in Nigeria,[5] where soil and climate are probably at their best in Africa, have shown that a cultivator can grow 600 kg. food crops on 1 hectare of land with only 300 hours work per year—that is to say, actual cultivation work; further labour will be needed for the periodic clearing and burning of fresh land. It might be added that the same amount of labour, applied to the same amount of land, would earn him enough money to buy 1500 kg. of grain if he grew cocoa and sold it—but this calls for a considerable capital investment several years in advance.

Nigerian conditions are, however, unusually good. There are many parts of Africa where it is necessary to work 600 or more hours to produce 600 kg. Even so, this is still a low total. The hours spent on farm work per cultivator per year in Africa seem to range from a minimum of 500 to a maximum of 1300. To this may be added up to 200 hours per year spent on non-farm work. But this is still low in relation to our average of 2000 hours per year, or the 3000 hours worked by our Victorian forbears.

The African cultivator has not read any textbooks on economics, but he understands (often better than those who govern him) very well the principle of "diminishing marginal returns to labour input under given conditions of technology". To return to the

[5] Galetti, Baldwin and Dina, *Nigerian Cocoa Farmers*, p. 337.

picture of a man with 1 hectare of land; if he spends only 300 hours per year cultivating it, he will obtain the 600 kg. of grain which constitute the minimum requirements for himself and one dependant. But supposing he is unwise enough, or unfortunate enough, to put 1000 hours of labour into the same hectare of land, he will find that each additional hour of labour is yielding him well under 1 kg. In the more adverse soil and climate of Gambia, at this labour input, the marginal return (further output obtained by working an extra hour of labour on the same land) is down to about one-third of a kilogram.[6]

Some careful measurements of African farm work have been made in Rhodesia.[7] The most vital labour inputs, obviously, are cultivation and harvesting. Weeding, though absolutely necessary, is nevertheless the form of labour input which yields diminishing returns. An additional hour's weeding was found to be worth only one-quarter to one-third kilogram of grain. In China and Japan, where clean weeding is practised to the extreme limit, this use of labour is nevertheless highly unremunerative. The marginal return, or further contribution to production, of some of their labour used for weeding is literally almost zero.

Stating the matter the other way round, the traditional Japanese style of farming, with 1½ to 2 men per hectare of cultivated land, is wasteful of labour,

[6] Haswell, *Economics of Agriculture in a Savannah Village*, Colonial Office Research Study No. 8, 1953.

[7] Massell and Johnson, Rand Corporation Publication R/443RC.

even though the land is double-cropped. In Taiwan even more densely populated agricultural land may be found, sometimes to the extreme extent of three men working half a hectare. In such a case, even with double-cropping, and the most careful mathematical planning of production,[8] they can only be occupied for about 75 days per year each. By this reckoning therefore it requires about 2 hectares to keep a man fully occupied.

Another interesting exercise in the mathematical planning of peasant farming, in this case in East Africa, was undertaken by Clayton.[9] A typical farm family in Kenya, also using hand cultivation methods to grow maize and tea, and to pasture dairy cattle (it would not have been worth their while to use a tractor even if one had been available, though Clayton recommends the hire of draught oxen for some of the season) had three able-bodied workers cultivating 4.3 hectares, or 1.43 hectares each. He was able to show how, by careful planning they could all keep themselves occupied throughout the year. By so doing they make the marginal return to labour fall, but not very seriously; it remains at 2.75 kg. of maize per hour, which is high for Africa.

Egypt represents an extreme case of high labour input, with only 0.6 hectares of agricultural land per man—76 per cent of this is double-cropped. The average Egyptian in 1960 worked 184 days per year (an improvement on the 168 days worked in 1955, brought about by the introduction of new and diversified crops). Paradoxically, the expansion of Egyptian

[8] Hsieh and Lee, World Population Conference, 1965.
[9] Journal of Agicultural Economics, May 1961.

agriculture is also checked by labour shortage. In this
case it is a shortage of women and children to do the
work which is customarily expected of them in the
planting season in June, and in the cotton-harvesting
season in September. The men are occupied to capacity
in the month of May only.[10] Probably it is the extension of education which is causing the shortage of
child labour. The obvious solution seems to be for the
men to do more of this work. However, it appears that
with agriculture at the Egyptian degree of sophistica-
tion, a man can be fully occupied on a hectare of land,
with sunshine and water as abundant as they are in
Egypt. This is confirmed by Egypt's historical evidence. In the late nineteenth century, when there was
about 1 hectare of cultivated land per man engaged in
agriculture, there was general complaint of labour
shortage.

Once you begin to use draught oxen, the area
which a man can cultivate is increased; or, conversely,
the amount of land which is required to keep him
fully occupied increases. Tarlok Singh, who later became Secretary of the Planning Commission for India,
developed an ingenious method[11] for estimating the
amount of land required to keep a man fully occupied
from information about the distribution of plough-
teams. He estimated it at 2.8 hectares for Bengal and
3.2 hectares for the other areas of good rainfall. And in
Bengal even this low figure (due in part to double-
cropping) must be qualified by the discovery by Ghosh

[10] Mona El Toms and Bent Hansen, *Seasonal Employment Profile in Egyptian Agriculture*, Institute of
National Planning Memorandum No. 501, 1964.
[11] *Poverty and Social Change*, 1945.

and Anakulchandra[12] that families in Bengal owning more than 0·5 hectare per person (about 1·5 hectares per man at work) were generally found leasing about a third of any land which they owned above this limit. Possibly they were devoting some of their time to non-agricultural activities. Even so this seems a very small lower limit for farm families using ox-ploughs.

In Indonesia, where some buffalo-ploughs are used, but much of the work is done by hand, the area of cultivated land per man in work is only about 0.6 hectare throughout the densely populated island of Java. In the outer islands, on the other hand, where the amount of land available per head of population is about 20 times what it is in Java, the amount of land cultivated per man still averages only about 1·3 hectares. Of this, half is left fallow each year, giving a harvested area per man about the same as in Java.

An interesting study by Shastri[13] on Indian agriculture in the Agra region showed that it was worth while for a cultivator growing wheat or sugar cane to put up to 1400 man-hours each year into a hectare of land. It was only after he exceeded this figure that the marginal return to labour began to fall. Even though he works very long hours in the monsoon season, it is doubtful whether the climate will permit the Indian farmer to work more than 2000 hours each year, however hard he tries. In the case of these two crops therefore, a holding of only 1½ hectares would keep him fully occupied. We may estimate a somewhat larger

[12] *Indian Journal of Agricultural Economics*, March 1950.

[13] *Indian Journal of Agricultural Economics*, Jan.–Mar. 1958.

holding if we allow for the lower labour requirements of other crops, and some fallow land. But Tarlok Singh's estimate of 3·2 hectares is probably quite high enough.

So there is a good deal of evidence that very large numbers of peasant cultivators throughout the world, living in densely populated areas, are content with the small areas which they farm, indeed could not conveniently manage more, with the implements and knowledge available to them. The amount they produce is very low. But do they want to produce more? They would have more income, but at the sacrifice of some of their leisure, and they may have their own ideas on this subject.

These ideas could not be more clearly expressed than they are in a tribal song on the subject of agricultural economics, which is admittedly an unusual subject, discovered by Fisk in a remote part of New Guinea. He proceeded to translate it into Australian.[14]

> "The primitive farmer says 'Cash
> Is unsatisfactory trash;
> It won't keep off rain
> And it gives me a pain
> If I use it to flavour my hash.
>
> So why should I work out my guts
> At the whim of these government mutts,
> My liquor comes free
> From the coconut tree
> And my Mary makes cups from the nuts.

[14] *Economic Record*, June 1964. Reproduced by permission of translator.

> Cash cropping is all very well
> If you've *got* to have something to sell;
> But tell me, sir, why
> If there is nothing to buy
> Should I bother? You can all go to hell.' "

We can find examples nearer home. Sir William Petty, writing about the Irish in 1691[15] complained: "What need have they to work, who can content themselves with *Potato's*, whereof the Labour of one Man can feed Forty?" Or, for that matter, the eighteenth-century English: "The manufacturing population do not labour above four days a week unless provisions happen to be very dear . . . when provisions are cheap they would not work above half the week, but sot or idle away half their time."[16]

The difficulty of persuading a poor peasant in India to give up some of his leisure can indeed be approximately expressed in quantitative form.[17] An unemployed man in an Indian village, and his dependents, will in fact be supported, at an absolute minimum subsistence level, by his relatives (probably on the understanding that he will support them if circumstances are reversed). He and his dependents will be consuming at a minimum rate amounting to about 1·8 kg. of grain per day. (The minimum food ration will be a little over 0·5 kg. grain-equivalent per person per day,

[15] *Political Arithmetick.*

[16] Temple, *Essays on Trade and Commerce* (quoted in Cunningham's Economic History).

[17] Estimates privately communicated by K. N. Raj, Director of the Agricultural Economics Research Centre, University of Delhi; original rupee values converted into grain at then prevailing prices.

and some allowance must be made for other consumption.) But he will not accept work, even in his own village, unless he is paid at the rate of approximately 3 kg. of grain per day. This latter figure indeed is not peculiar to India; a most extensive review of information all over the world, and back into the historic past in Europe, shows that the minimum wage for hired labour for farm work in the village never falls below this figure of 3 kg. of grain-equivalent per day. But to persuade an unemployed Indian peasant to work away from his village, with travelling expenses, additional expenses for housing, costs and difficulties of being separated from his family, etc., will require the offer of a wage of at least 5 kg. of grain-equivalent per day.

In other words, leisure has a real value even to very poor people. They will not work harder and produce more unless they are offered substantially increased earnings, and also an adequate supply of goods at reasonable prices on which to spend them. (We will leave aside the harsh expedient, introduced into many parts of Africa by European imperial administrators, and subsequently kept in force by African governments, of imposing taxes which have to be paid in money, as a way of compelling such cultivators either to produce more, or else to go out and seek paid employment.) Farmers are indeed unwilling to work for money which will not buy anything; they do not suffer from "money illusion" in the way that many better-educated urban workers seem to suffer. In India there is a fair supply of goods available in exchange for farmers who do earn additional money. The abundance of low-priced industrial goods in Japan, at an early stage in that country's development, probably played an important part in inducing Japanese farmers to produce more.

But additional earnings, and an adequate choice of goods on which to spend them, are not the whole story. There is another factor so fundamental, which in our own world we so much tend to take for granted, that there is a danger of our forgetting it, and that is transport. It is no use expecting the farmer to produce more than is needed to meet his family's consumption requirements, and perhaps for some exchange within his own village with local craftsmen and traders, unless he can get the surplus to a market, which may be a considerable distance from the village. To take an extreme example, the Royal Commission of 1953–55 reported that there were some parts of East Africa where the only way to get grain out of the village for sale in the market was by head-loading. To carry a ton of grain for 1 kilometre the porters made a charge of 12 kg. of grain. Suppose that the market was 40 kilometres away from the village, as it well might have been. In this case the farmer would have lost half of the value of the grain simply by the process of carrying it to market. He certainly will not grow much grain for sale under these circumstances.

It is because of transport difficulties that we get the rather paradoxical consequence of some of the poorest and remotest agricultural communities in the world working hard to grow difficult crops like cotton and tobacco. The porter's charge per ton remains the same as before, but the value per ton of the crop delivered to market is much higher, so there is more chance of the farmer being able to stand the transport cost.

These East African costs were admittedly exceptional. Surprisingly, it is because the agriculture of East Africa is comparatively productive that the porters require to be paid so much. The median value of head porterage charges throughout the world is about 8½ kg. grain equivalent per ton-kilometre transported, and in China, where everyone is poorer, the charge is only about 4½ kg. Even these charges however are quite high enough to prevent any farmer sending grain to market for more than a few kilometres.

Where you have no roads, and are too poor even to keep draught animals, head porterage is the only possible form of transport; and travellers are indeed amazed at the skill with which Africans and Asians can balance heavy loads on the tops of their heads. The next step forward is to use pack animals, which still do not require any roads, other than rough tracks—but of course this is only possible for people who are able to feed them. In East Africa, pack animal transport is almost as expensive as head-loading, because it is so difficult to protect the animals from fly-borne diseases. The median world charge for pack animal transport is 4 kg. of grain per ton-kilometre of transport, and the lowest charges are in the Middle East, where the camel, which is a very economical performer (though it does not look it) gives transport costing only 2 kg. per ton-kilometre. In China, pack animals, with their demands for food which look excessive by Chinese standards, cannot compete with human porters. Also, when it comes to really steep slopes, it is found that the human porter can work at lower cost than the pack animal. This was true of traffic carried over the Alps in mediaeval Europe, and is true of loads carried up steep slopes to the military outposts in Hong Kong today.

Though not so prohibitive in cost as head-loading, pack animal transport is nevertheless pretty discouraging to production and trade. The next advance is to build roads and to use wagons drawn by horses or oxen. But on the very bad roads which are still found in many parts of the world, and which also prevailed among our predecessors until the late eighteenth century, this only brought about a moderate reduction in transport costs. Wagon transport was however practicable over longer distances for the early settlers in America and Australia, where food for horses was abundant.

We always tend to assume that the whole western world had entered the Railway Age by the middle of the nineteenth century. It comes as a surprise therefore to find that as late as 1920 there were about 1.3 million hectares of good agricultural land in the American Middle West[18] still lying undeveloped and used for grazing only, because it was more than 130 kilometres from railway. To transport grain for this distance by horse-wagon would have required a round trip lasting 4 to 6 days, and the cost, at the rates of wages then prevailing, would have exceeded the entire selling value of the grain by 20 to 30 per cent. So this large productive area remained uncultivated until the advent of motor transport in the 1920s. The planners of railways in the West Australian wheat

[18] Thorn, World Population Conference, 1954.

belt[19] assumed that 20 kilometres was the maximum distance over which a settler could be expected to carry his wheat by horse-wagon.

There are very large areas in the world today, just as there were in our own past history, where any improvement of agriculture is almost completely blocked by inadequacy of transport to take the produce to market. If we want to help some of the poorest people in the world to produce more, we must ensure that they have markets in which they can sell their agricultural produce and buy something valuable in exchange. But most of all, we must help to provide them with transport.

[19] See *Economic Record*, December 1963, p. 474.

5

Buying and Selling

THROUGHOUT THE world there are so many millions of poor people who, even if not actually hungry, are living on a diet so incomparably worse than our own that the thought comes naturally to us—should we not give them some of the food which we seem able to produce so abundantly? Examination of the cost, not only of purchasing the food, but also of transporting it and distributing it in the remote areas where it is most wanted, together with consideration of the amount of taxation which we are already paying, may lead us to have second thoughts about such a proposal. But at any rate, we go on to say, surely we could sell them some of our surplus food, maybe at a concessional price? It is natural to suggest this. But there is one fatal objection. How are they to pay for it? They cannot pay for it in borrowed money—at least they could not go on doing so for long. It comes as a shock to us to realise that there is only one thing which these poor countries have to sell, and that is agricultural produce—either food itself, or products such as cotton and coffee, which make use of the same land and labour as does their food production.

It is harder still for us to grasp the important point, that, this being so, our persistence in subsidising the production of high-cost food surpluses in North America and Western Europe, so far from aiding the poor countries, is making their position very much worse by flooding the world markets in which they might have hoped to sell some of their agricultural output.

To examine the situation more closely, let us remind ourselves again that (expressing all other agricultural products in terms of their economic wheat-equivalent) 250 kg. of wheat-equivalent per person per year represents the necessary physiological minimum of consumption. It will also be remembered how we have traced the pace of agricultural progress by measuring productivity per head of the farm population in the same units. When production is at or near subsistence level it is naturally all consumed. But it does not have to rise very far above subsistence level before the farmer begins selling some of his output. He rates some other objects of consumption as more urgent than a further increase in his food consumption.

This situation is illustrated by a diagram of the production and food expenditure of a number of farm families in the Punjab (a region wealthier and more productive than the Indian average).

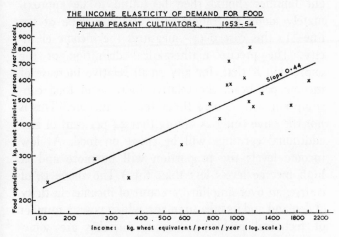

THE INCOME ELASTICITY OF DEMAND FOR FOOD
PUNJAB PEASANT CULTIVATORS , 1953-54

Food expenditure: kg. wheat equivalent / person / year (log. scale)

Slope 0.44

Income: kg. wheat equivalent / person / year (log. scale)

(It will be observed that both the horizontal and vertical scales are logarithmic; the relationships can be most clearly observed in this way.)

In this village the productivity of one family (probably because of illness or other misfortune) was below subsistence level. The family's consumption was at subsistence level, sustained presumably by sale of assets, or borrowing or gifts from neighbours. As productivity rose, food consumption also increased, though much less rapidly. The most successful family in the village had an average production per head of about eight times subsistence level; but food consumption per head had only risen 2·4 times above subsistence level.

This relationship is known as the "income elasticity of demand for food". The best method of measuring it is to draw a diagram with logarithmic scales both for per head production and for per head food consumption. The points representing the different families should then be found to lie approximately along a straight line, and the slope of the line—in this case 0·44—measures the income elasticity. The precise mathematical definition of the expression is that, for any small relative increase of income per head, the relative increase of food consumption will be 0·44 times that of income. (This is not the same thing as saying that 44 per cent of any additional earnings will be spent on food. At low income levels the proportion will be more and at high income levels less than this.) The above is, of course, an over-simplified account of income elasticity of demand and its measurement, which poses a number of technical problems. Serious mistakes are sometimes made by trying to relate changes in consumption to short-period changes in income—people take some time to settle down into new consumption habits when their incomes change, whether upwards or downwards. Also it is not safe to assume that the coefficient of income elasticity of demand will be the same at all levels of income. For food, taken as a whole, income elasticity falls off at higher income levels. For some foods it falls off very much faster— the demand for cereals and sugar, for instance, becomes saturated at comparatively low income levels.

Subject to these warnings, however, and bearing in mind that we are at present only concerned with food consumption by comparatively poor families, we may review the available information. The figure for Punjab seems to be fairly representative of peasant agricultural communities. A similar figure was obtained for irrigation farmers in Iraq. In poorer communities, however, the figure is much higher. Both China and Vietnam have shown figures of 0·7. That is to say, if production rises, a much larger proportion of the increased product will be kept by farm families for their consumption than is the case in Punjab.

Increments of income must necessarily be spent on increased consumption of one object or another, or saved. The abundance and cheapness of other objects for consumption may lower the farmer's income elasticity of demand for food, and increase his income elasticity of demand for industrial products. Different farm communities may also have very different ideas about the possibility or desirability of saving. Conversely, shortage of industrial goods may raise the income elasticity of demand for food. Finally, food consumption is not, as some people have mistakenly supposed, simply a determinate response to physiological need. There are very considerable social elements in food consumption, in all countries—it is always very painful not to be able to follow the established social customs of one's neighbours.

All these considerations have to be borne in mind when we examine the available information. The highest income elasticity of demand for food ever recorded was, unexpectedly, found among English agricultural labourers of the eighteenth century. The social customs of eighteenth-century England favoured hearty eating and drinking, when one could afford it; there were few industrial products to be had, at any rate within reach of the farm labourer; and there was little purpose in his saving, because he knew that the Poor Law would reduce his allowance correspondingly when he was in trouble.

Very low income elasticity of demand for food, on the other hand, is found among Japanese farmers. Several factors are at work here. The Japanese have, more than any other nation in the world (except perhaps the Chinese, when permitted to do so), a strong desire to save, often in order to enable them to start a small business. Industrial products are cheap and abundant in rural markets. Finally, social customs do not favour hearty eating. The wealthy Japanese takes pride in consuming rice, raw fish and vegetables in just the same manner as his poorer neighbours.

Another example of exceptionally low income elasticity of demand for food is found among African tribesmen working temporarily in industrial towns in Zambia. These men have an extremely strong urge to save, perhaps even to the detriment of their health, so as to be able to purchase some durable consumer goods and return to their villages as soon as possible.

Urban India, on the other hand, has a higher income elasticity of demand for food than rural India. This does not mean that urban families eat more than rural families of a similar income level in the simple sense of the words—in fact, measured in calories and proteins, they consume less. What it does mean is that Indian urban families buy their food in the more expensive forms—dairy products, sugar, fruit, meat, etc. The explanation for this can only be sociological. The coefficient of income elasticity of demand for food in urban India appears to be about 0·7 as against 0·4 in rural India.

It is interesting to observe also the income elasticity of demand for objects other than food in India. The highest is for jewellery, where the coefficient is over 2 (i.e. for a 1 per cent increase in income, expenditure on jewellery goes up by more than 2 per cent). The Indian however regards jewellery predominantly as a form of saving, and only indirectly as a form of consumption. A coefficient of 2·0 also applies to silk clothing, 1·8 to wool, but only 0·8 to cotton clothing. Household equipment also stands high at 1·9, education at 1·8, and medicine at 1·5. The coefficient for housing is 1·3 in the country and 1·15 in the town, and for furniture about 1·5.

These figures give us an indication of what poor families—it is probably much the same throughout the world—regard as their urgent needs. Except for the very poorest, food is a comparatively less urgent need. It is not for us to criticise their standards, but to help them to fulfil them. This will mean—let us repeat the unexpected conclusion—being willing to *buy* more agricultural produce from them, and to sell them in exchange the goods which they want, or the materials and equipment for making them.

6

The Advance of Agriculture

MAIZE IS the crop frequently grown by "cut and burn" cultivators. In Chapter 2, we saw that the yields may sometimes be as high as 2 tons to the hectare on the very best soils when recently cleared, falling however in most cases quite quickly to 600 kg. (0·6 tons) per hectare, at which point the farmers usually decide to abandon the cultivation, and to clear fresh land. On the poorer soils and in the drier climates they generally grow millet or sorghum, where yields may be even lower. In 1964–6, the average African yield of maize was 1050 kg. per hectare, of sorghum 780, and of millet 560.

The cultivation of wheat in thirteenth-century England is estimated to have given a yield as low as 430 kg. per hectare.[1] The amount required for seed (at that time broadcast, not drilled) stood at 170 kg. per hectare, leaving a very poor net return. A similar figure was estimated for Russia in the fifteenth century, remaining unchanged until the nineteenth.[2]

Wheat yields in England showed a gradual improvement. According to Richardson, the yield had risen to 1 ton per hectare by the middle of the sixteenth century, though M. K. Bennett[3] thought the rise came later. The same level was reached by France and Germany about the end of the eighteenth century, though the well managed estate of von Thünen in Mecklenburg (the subject of an important contemporary economic treatise) showed for all crops yields about double the average German level.

[1] Richardson, *Outlook on Agriculture*, Winter 1960.
[2] Official estimate made in 1869, quoted *Agricultural History*, Jan. 1960, pp. 6–7.
[3] *Economic History*, Vol. 3.

It is interesting to see, in the light of the discussion in Chapter 3 of Ester Boserup's study, that agriculture is capable of retrogression. Mid-nineteenth-century Greece had wheat yields of only about 460 kg. per hectare, whereas we have sufficient information to show[4] that the yield in the ancient world was twice this level. In ancient Egypt, the yield was as high as 1·9 tons per hectare. Indeed it was probably only the attaining of these yields in a compact area of land which made the ancient Egyptian civilisation possible. At some period between the beginning of the Christian Era and the nineteenth century, we know that there was a heavy reduction of population in Egypt. In the 1830s wheat yields had fallen to 1·4 tons to the hectare, and did not recover to the level of the ancient world until the 1930s.

In the case of rice, it is very easy to become confused about the unit of measurement. The outer husk of the rice is not under any circumstances edible; but there is considerable difference of opinion about how much else should be milled away, giving final yields ranging from 72 per cent down to 60 per cent of the original. All the measures quoted below are therefore in terms of rough rice. There is some evidence that in China, as long ago as the eleventh century, the yield had been raised to 2·3 tons per hectare, while in Japan, still a comparatively primitive country, it was only 0·9 tons per hectare at that time. Japan reached 1·4 tons by the sixteenth century and 1·7 tons by the time of the Meiji Restoration, which began the modernisation of Japan in the 1870s. China in the eleventh century also made an important genetic

[4] Michell, *The Economics of Ancient Greece.*

discovery, namely breeding a quick-ripening rice, which made possible the extension of rice cultivation into more northerly latitudes than had hitherto been possible; this discovery made all the difference to China's population and economic progress. Further progress however was to be slow; by the 1930s the yield was still only 2·5 tons of rough rice per hectare. There are a number of countries in Asia and Africa where the yield is still only 1 ton per hectare. In Japan, on the other hand, the yield is now 5 tons, and even higher yields have been obtained in a small rice-growing area in Spain.

Up to the 1930s, it is seen from the table, improvements in yield were taking place, but they were slow. Some countries—Canada, USA, South Africa and India—were indeed slipping back, in comparison with the 1909–13 figure. Striking improvements in yield began almost everywhere in the 1940s. Many of these were based upon knowledge—the hybridisation of maize is the most striking example—which had been discovered earlier, but which farmers had not previously had the means or the will to apply.

The interpretation of the Indian figures is always difficult, because of year-by-year climatic variations. One should never reach any conclusion on the figures of a single year, and should always take an average of at least three years. Even this does not always suffice. India suffered from the unusual misfortune of a bad monsoon in two succeeding years, 1965 and 1966. In 1967 agricultural production rose by no less than 14 per cent above the average for the three-year period 1964–66 shown in the table. This again, however, is a figure for a single year, and too much weight should not be attached to it. Many people are now as excessively optimistic about Indian agricultural prospects as they were excessively pessimistic two years ago. It still remains permissible, however, to be

Crop yields in tons per hectare

	1885–89	1909–13	1934–38	1964–66
MAIZE				
USA	1·65	1·63	1·40	4·37
Italy		1·58	2·06	3·49
Argentine		1·36	1·81	1·88
S. Africa		0·86	0·83	0·96
Philippines		0·66	0·61	0·67
USSR		1·11	1·50	2·62
WHEAT				
France	1·18	1·32	1·56	3·08
UK	2·03	2·13	2·31	4·05
Canada	0·99	1·33	0·71	1·59
USA	0·71	0·98	0·87	1·76
Argentine	0·67	0·62	0·98	1·44
India	0·65	0·81	0·69	0·82
Australia	0·52	0·81	0·80	1·30
USSR		0·81	0·83	1·13
China			1·06	0·84
RICE (unmilled weight)				
Italy		3·28	5·30	4·64
Spain		4·99	6·23	6·17
Burma		1·56	1·41	1·61
Ceylon		1·24	0·99	1·87
India		1·13	1·36	1·40
Indonesia		1·69	1·58	1·81
Japan		3·07	3·63	5·02
Pakistan			1·48	1·63
Philippines		0·73	1·09	1·30
Taiwan		1·70	2·46	3·73
Thailand		1·58	1·29	1·63
Egypt		3·56	3·49	4·45
USA		1·70	2·47	4·73
China			2·77	2·69

NOTE: the figures for China refer to 1928–33 and to 1957 respectively.

moderately optimistic about the improving trend of Indian agricultural productivity.

Many factors have been at work to bring about this sudden and dramatic improvement in agricultural productivity, which has been almost world-wide since the 1940s. The breeding of hybrid maize, which has already been mentioned, is only one of the most dramatic of the improvements in plant genetics which are always being made. People who hope for a "breakthrough" in this field, or some new strain of seed which can be distributed throughout the developing world, are however likely to be disappointed. Genetic improvement generally proceeds by gradual stages, in response to years of hard work, and, "breakthroughs" are very rare. Moreover strains of plants are extraordinarily sensitive to small differences in climate. A strain which may be developed successfully at one place may prove quite unsuccessful at another only 200 miles away. However, even the most cautious cannot now deny that a new strain of wheat recently bred in Mexico, and of rice bred in the Philippines, look like proving successful in India and Pakistan, and raising yields by a factor of 50 per cent or more.

Next after genetics may be mentioned improved cultural practices. Tractors plough faster and more thoroughly than draught animals. Herbicides check weed growth more effectively and cheaply than additional cultivation. But probably the most important factor has been the greatly increased use of fertiliser. The very high rice yields for some countries shown in the table are conditional upon unusually heavy fertiliser inputs.

The response of plants to fertiliser, like the response of children to cake, is a true case of diminishing returns. Those who have been deprived of it, on first receiving a moderate quantity, enjoy it enormously. Succeeding increments have less effect. Whether a point is eventually reached where further intake of fertiliser can be expected to reduce the plant's growth is a matter of discussion, though this undoubtedly does occur under certain circumstances.

The results of literally thousands of experiments are now available showing the effects of fertiliser on plants. The most convenient general summary is in the Crowther-Yates equation and diagram. In other words, it is where fertilisers have been hitherto least used that they will do most good.

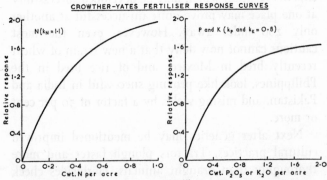

CROWTHER–YATES FERTILISER RESPONSE CURVES

The form of the response curve is $Y = Y_0 + d\,(1 - 10^{-kX})$, where Y is the yield with a fertiliser dressing of X cwt. N, P_2O_5 or K_2O per acre, Y_0 the yield with no fertiliser, d the limiting response, and k a value assumed to be constant for each of the three principal classes of fertiliser. From 'Fertiliser Policy in War-time' by E. M. Crowther and F. Yates (Empire Journal of Experimental Agriculture, April 1941)

The following table shows the expected effect of each unit of fertiliser used in India.

Response to Fertilisers in India
(tons additional grain/ton of nutrient supplied)

	Rice (unmilled)	Wheat	Maize	US price $/ton nutrient
Nitrogen				
at 22 kg./ha.	11·7	10·5	10·7	152
at 45 kg./ha.	8·6	8·9		
Phosphorus pentoxide				
at 22 kg./ha.	9·4	7·6	6·2	95
World prices including freight) $/ton grain	107	73	61	

On the right-hand side of the table are shown the prices at which fertiliser could be bought. As there are a number of different forms of fertiliser, it is most convenient to express the prices per unit of the actual nutrient, nitrogen, phosphorus pentoxide, etc. Thus the most frequently used nitrogenous fertiliser, sulphate of ammonia, contains 20 per cent of nitrogen. The price of sulphate of ammonia is one-fifth of that indicated in the table per unit of nitrogen element. The prices quoted are for where the fertilisers can be obtained most cheaply in the world, at works in the USA or Japan.

The expected responses from each unit of fertiliser input are taken from the summary by Dr Sukhatme,[5] Director of Statistics for FAO, based on a large number of Indian experiments.

The table should be read as follows. Take first the minimum prices given to the right of the table. Then make your own allowance for the cost of transporting

[5] *Feeding India's Growing Millions.*

the fertiliser to India and distributing it there. Double the at-works price, or even multiply by three if you wish. Then divide your result by the coefficients shown in the body of the table for crop response to each unit of fertiliser. In this way we calculate the cost in dollars of producing an additional ton of wheat, rice, etc., by means of fertiliser, taking into account not only the cost of fertiliser at works, but also its transport and distribution. Then compare these costs with the prices which India has been having to pay for imported grains (including transport). The saving is enormous. Financially speaking, quite apart from any humanitarian considerations, putting fertiliser on to Indian agricultural land must be about the best investment in the world. Why has it not been done already? This is indeed a sad story. Those in charge of Indian affairs are now willing to admit, in private at any rate, that there has been a considerable degree of incompetence and irrationality in their decisions. Fertilisers, they decided, were so important that they could not possibly import them, but must make them themselves. This was an unwise decision; because the making of nitrogenous fertilisers, of the sort principally required, makes huge demands upon capital, and upon highly skilled workers and technicians, which India can ill afford to meet. But in any case, India fell far short even of providing the planned quantity of fertilisers. When it came to the point, and there was a shortage of electric power, steelworks were given priority over fertilisers.

It is not a case of the enlightened administrator having to force fertilisers upon the reluctant peasant. It is almost the reverse. Indian farmers may not be able to read the technical journals, but they now know very well how productive fertiliser can be on their soils. The available supplies are rationed by a cumbrous bureaucratic procedure, and Indian farmers are happily paying black-market prices in order to get more than their quota.

To raise Indian rice yields to Japanese levels, however, will require more than fertiliser. The application of more than a moderate quantity of nitrogenous fertilisers to Indian rice causes it to "fall prostrate", as one Japanese observer put it. Genetic work will have to go hand in hand with increased input of fertiliser, to produce rice with shorter and stiffer stalks, which can stand the increased weight of the heads.

It is an over-simplification to show the responses to nitrogen, phosphorus and potash separately, and to imply that if you put them all on together you will get a response equal to the sum of the specific responses. In fact, by a judicious mixing of fertilisers, it may be possible to get a combined response substantially better than the sum of the individual responses. Farmers, experimenters and mathematicians all have a good deal more work to do before we can reach final conclusions on this interesting subject. One extraordinarily encouraging example of such a combined response was obtained in Rhodesia.[6] Starting with maize yielding 450 kg. per hectare—about the lowest rate conceivable—the experimenters applied 25 tons per hectare of animal manure (containing only 0·6 per cent nitrogen, and small quantities of other nutrients), together with a chemical

[6] Johnson, *Rhodesia Agricultural Journal*, July–August 1962.

fertiliser (urea) supplying nitrogen element up to the rate of 89 kg. per hectare. Per unit of nitrogen applied, the response was not 12 units of grain as in India, but no less than 32. Agricultural scientists familiar with the peculiar deficiencies of African soils accept this result.

The same principle is seen in reverse in the results of some experiments which show that, in certain soils, heavy applications of nitrogen not supplemented by potash may lead to an actual reduction of yield. The principle source of potash exports is Germany, and several German scientists have been at work, quite justifiably, in pointing out these relationships.

An even more dramatic example has been found in English dairy farming. Cows fed on crops of grass obtained from heavy fertilisation with nitrogen, if it has not been supplemented with magnesium, may develop a deficiency of magnesium in their circulation which may cause them to collapse and die within a few hours.

It is of course important for the world to produce more grains, which provide adequate if uninteresting diets for hungry peoples. But much of the grain which we already produce, particularly the maize, is going to feed livestock. As the world advances, we should expect to see people consuming more meat, eggs and milk, some of which may be produced by feeding grains to livestock, some from grass. Until recently, we thought of grass just as something which grew. The idea of deliberately cultivating and fertilising it is something new. This has played a principal part in the extremely high agricultural productivity of New Zealand. A New Zealand farmer once took me to the top of a hill the view covering a wide expanse of country. "For as far as you can see", he said, "there is not a blade of indigenous grass left. The whole country has been re-seeded and fertilised."

Unlike a crop of grain, which can be precisely weighed, it is much more difficult to measure the yield of grass. It is no use leaving it to grow to the end of the season, when it will have long since gone to seed and lost most of its value. The experimenter has to crop it at intervals whose length is still the subject of dispute. Most of the weight of the grass cropped by the cow or by the experimenter consists of water, the proportion varying with the season. Results therefore all have to be expressed dryweight (sometimes this is converted to "starch equivalent", which is lower, omitting some of the lignin and other substances deemed indigestible by livestock).

It would be impossible for any farmer to keep enough livestock to eat all the grass which grows in the early summer. This of course is the reason why farmers have to make hay, to conserve some of this growth for winter use. Traditional methods of hay-making are estimated to waste 45 per cent of the carbohydrate and 32 per cent of the protein in the grass. As anyone can observe, haymaking is now progressively giving place to silage made with acid or molasses, which reduces the wastage to 22 per cent and 10 per cent respectively. Wastage is reduced to a minimum (5 per cent for carbohydrate and 7 per cent for protein) when grass is dried in an oven as soon as it has been cut. This method, which is of course more costly than silage-making in terms of labour and fuel, is frequently used for grass cut from airfields, playgrounds, etc., and provides a valuable protein food for poultry and other livestock.

Yields of British grasslands vary greatly.[7] The so-called "rough grazings", with which the country is abundantly supplied, yield only 2.2 tons of dry weight per hectare per year, of which only 40 per cent is starch equivalent. The average cultivated grass (leys) yields 6.7 tons dry weight, of which 50 per cent is starch equivalent. On the best leys, and also on the best permanent grass, the yield rises to 9 tons and 60 per cent starch equivalent. The "rough grazings", Davis scornfully remarked, are still about as productive as they were when they were breeding deer and rabbits for our ancestors to hunt.

Grass thoroughly enjoys a cool and rainy climate, and in Great Britain yields are probably highest in Scotland. The grass plant is very shallow-rooted, in comparison with the cereals, and is very sensitive even to a temporary shortage of moisture.

An interesting diagram can be prepared showing the response of grass to fertiliser.

The English experiments, it will be seen, began with fairly low-yielding pasture. A grass-clover mixture gives a much higher yield, mainly because clover is one of the plants which has the capacity for fixing nitrogen from the atmosphere. The symbiotic nodules on the roots of the clover plants, however, seem to dislike chemical competition, and restrict their activities when nitrogenous fertiliser is applied.

The high yields in Scotland, of 9 tons dry matter

[7] Davis, International Grassland Conference, Reading, 1960.

to the hectare, served as a starting point for experiments showing the effect of fertilisation with nitrogen, which could raise the yield to 15 tons of dry matter to the hectare—the highest in Europe—but no further.

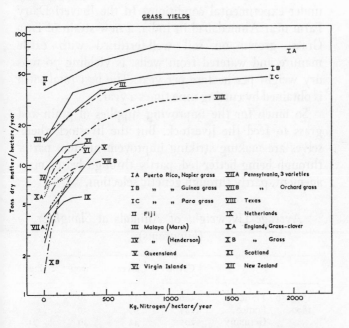

GRASS YIELDS

IA Puerto Rico, Napier grass
IB   "   "   Guinea grass
IC   "   "   Para grass
II Fiji
III Malaya (Marsh)
IV   "   (Henderson)
V Queensland
VI Virgin Islands
VIIA Pennsylvania, 3 varieties
VIIB   "   Orchard grass
VIII Texas
IX Netherlands
XA England, Grass-clover
XB   "   Grass
XI Scotland
XII New Zealand

Tons dry matter/hectare/year
Kg. Nitrogen/hectare/year

Dutch scientists, with a climate less rainy than ours, think that it is necessary for farmers to aim at a minimum of 7–10 tons of dry matter per hectare per year from their grassland, if they wish to prevent soil deterioration.

In the tropics, however, both the amount of nitrogenous fertiliser which grass can take before showing seriously diminishing returns, and the ultimate yields of dry matter obtained, are of a completely different order of magnitude from those of temperate climates. The maximum temperate yield is 15 tons dry matter per hectare, the maximum tropical yield exactly 5 times as much, or 75 tons.

This latter is not just a result obtainable only under experimental conditions. In the Jhaveri Dairy Farm near Ahmedabad in India, a new strain of Pusa Grass, grown on soil well-fertilised with cattle manure and watered from wells, is yielding 70 tons dry weight per hectare per year. The best total yield is obtained by cutting nine times a year.

So much for the improving supplies of grain and grass to feed the livestock. But the livestock themselves are making striking improvements too, partly through being better fed, partly through better management, partly through genetic selection.

Average Liveweight of Animals at Slaughter (kilograms)

		Cattle	Calves	Sheep	Pigs
1750–56	France	200	35	20	—
1800	France	245	65	20	—
	Germany	205	42	30	71
1860–70	France	410	86	36	126
	Germany	335	51	36	101
	England	463	75	50	59
1925	Germany	420	91	44	140
	England	515	87	54	103
1961	Germany	504	84	—	111
	England	488	55	58	88
	USA	459	105	—	108
	Yugoslavia	251	75	21	93
	Taiwan	258	—	—	88
	S. Africa	281	30	24	59
	N. Zealand	388	38	47	69

The animals slaughtered for meat in eighteenth-century France (and in the rest of Europe they were probably worse) were small and skinny. The present standards of Yugoslavia and Taiwan are comparable with those of France at the beginning of the nineteenth century. In such countries the supply of beef, it must be remembered, comes from draught oxen and milch cows which have reached the end of their useful careers. In Voivodina, the most prosperous part of Yugoslavia, where horses and not cattle are used as draught animals, the average weight of cattle for slaughter is 550 kg., as high as anywhere in Europe. Beef from old draught oxen can also be remarkably tough. It was the cessation of the use of oxen for draught power, which came in England about 1780, rather later in Scotland, which made possible the legend of "the Roast Beef of Old England"; which in the nineteenth century was probably plumper and more tender than that of the Continent. But all good things must come to an end; the taste for fat beef began to turn down about the 1920s. The United States slaughters its cattle smaller than does Europe, but breeds fat veal. New Zealand, dependent on export sales, is now slaughtering its meat considerably younger. The taste for fat pork also seems to have reached its all-time maximum in Germany in the 1920s. Mutton, however, does not seem to be seriously affected by slimming fashions.

Besides these improvements in the quantity and quality of meat, farmers have also been able to fatten their beasts more quickly and turn them over more rapidly. Between 1862 and 1909 the average age at slaughter in France fell from 8·0 to 4·6 years for cattle, 3·0 to 2·2 for sheep and 1·2 to 0·85 for pigs. Modern cattle breeders are trying to bring the age of slaughter down to a little over 2 years, though to the detriment of the taste of the meat, as many think. As for pigs, the output per year in the United States is about one and a half times the pig population at any one moment, i.e. an average time for maturing of only two-thirds of a year.

Likewise there have been great improvements in the performance of dairy cows. The natural unit for measuring the output of milk is the lactation, which lasts for about 250 days. It is, however, more convenient to measure yields per year. These are affected by the farmer's skill in having his cows calving at the right time, and of having food supplies available. The average cow in India yields only about 240 kg. of milk per year, of which about 70 are sucked by the calf. An output as low as this probably does not repay the value of the fodder which the cow consumes. But the Indian is willing to put up with a negative economic return for religious reasons. For him it is sacrilegious to kill an old cow, however unproductive. Among commercial cow keepers, yields as low as 750 kg. have been reported from Bulgaria and Greece. A German estimate for 1800 gives 860 kg., with only a slight improvement in the first half of the nineteenth century. Denmark, which was later to become a world leader in dairy farming, in 1861 still had a yield at only about this level.

Cows may live entirely on grass, silage and hay; or they may also be fed "concentrates" i.e. various grains, and other feeding stuffs high in protein, such as oilseed cake. There is still a good deal of uncer-

Milk yields in tons per cow per year

	1870–1880	1890–1900	1911–1913	1934–1938	1950–1952	1964–1965
Netherlands	—	—	—	3·47	3·76	4·20
Denmark	1·24	2·12	2·62	3·13	3·36	3·09
Belgium	—	—	—	3·18	3·40	3·88
US	—	1·65	—	1·95	2·78	3·63
Germany	1·30	1·75	2·20	2·48	2·62	3·61
Sweden	1·01	1·28	1·77	2·38	2·93	3·54
New Zealand	—	1·69	—	2·58	2·62	2·91
France	—	1·65	—	1·78	1·87	2·88
UK	1·77	1·87	—	2·53	2·78	2·68
Australia	—	—	1·47	2·10	2·42	2·34

tainty about the additional yield of milk which can be obtained from a given cow in given circumstances by feeding her a given amount of concentrates. It must be borne in mind that Australia, New Zealand and Ireland are producing low-priced dairy products for export, and under their circumstances the feeding of concentrates is hardly ever worth while. Even though they might improve the yield of milk, the proceeds would fall short of the cost. Every farmer, however, knows that cows are animals of remarkable individuality; and recent research has shown that there are great differences between individual cows in their capacity to make good use of concentrates. Improvements in milk yields therefore depends largely on genetic selection, which must be a very slow business in an animal so slow-breeding. Even so, some striking improvements have been possible in a short time, as is seen by the figures for the US, France and Germany.

It is now easier to understand how the world is

running into an embarrassing surplus of dairy products.

In the case of pigs, bringing the animals to maturity earlier, good management, and also genetic selection have brought about very large economies in requirements of feeding stuffs. To produce 1 kg. (liveweight) of pigmeat required 6 kg. of feed in 1913, 5 in the 1920s, 4 in the 1950s, and a considerably lower figure now prevails among the best modern breeders. A kilogram of poultry meat liveweight can be produced from only 2½ kg. of feed.

In bringing about these improvements, reduction in animal diseases has also played an important part. Since antibiotics became cheap and abundant during the last decade, animal feeders have included them in the rations, with immediately beneficial effects. Microbiologists point out however that the widespread use of antibiotics in this way is very likely to breed strains of micro-organisms resistant to antibiotics, and that later these may directly infect, or have means of transferring their infectivity to, other micro-organisms, to cause devastating epidemics, against which antibiotics would be of no avail. From this particular method of increasing agricultural productivity we should beat a quick retreat, if we have any sense.

Besides the advance in the quantity of produce obtainable from each unit of land or livestock, we are also interested in measuring the advances in the amount produced by each man engaged in agriculture. So far we have looked only at the primitive cultivator, who may be producing less than he might be capable of producing, and whose economy has often remained unchanged over very long periods of time. When people complain of the slowness of the rate of advance in simple peasant societies, with production only about keeping pace with population growth, they should bear in mind De Vries's generalisation, that we should regard it as the law of nature that in such communities the rate of population growth and the rate of increase in agricultural production must be almost the same. For, if either exceeds the other, very serious consequences immediately ensue. Agricultural output is so low, leaving so small a margin over minimum physiological requirements, that if population increases without an increase in agricultural production, there will be famine. But the converse also holds. Such communities have only the minimum provisions for transport and marketing. If agricultural production increased appreciably faster than population, there would be an unsaleable surplus which would wreck what frail commercial economy there is.

Consider even eighteenth-century France, probably the most civilised part of the world at that time, though based on an agriculture of low productivity. Agricultural production was increasing only 0.5 per cent per year, as compared with a rate of population growth of 0.2 per cent per year. Even in nineteenth-century Germany, at any rate up to 1880, still predominantly a country of small peasant farmers, the rate of population growth was 0.8 per cent per year, and the rate of increase of agricultural production only 1.1 per cent per year.

In no country was there any clearly marked dividing line between these older and less productive types of agriculture and modern commercial farming. Everywhere it was a process taking place by gradual degrees. It must be remembered that we are still thinking of a time (before the 1940s) when the most advanced methods of cultivation still depended upon a team of horses, fertilisers were scarce, and antibiotics unknown. From the mid-nineteenth century to the 1930s there was a considerable uniformity of experience in all the advanced countries, with the quantity of produce obtained per man engaged in agriculture rising at the rate of about 1½ per cent per year. This progress took the form of improvements to some farms, and also of the closing down of some of the less successful farms and their absorption by their neighbours.

As things were up to the beginning of the 1940s, there were some grounds for expecting that the world was going to face some difficulty in feeding itself, even at the slow rates of population growth then prevailing, and that the price of food was likely to rise relative to the price of other products. But the acceleration of the pace of agricultural improvement which came quite suddenly during the decade of the 1940s has completely altered the outlook, in spite of the great increase in the rate of growth of world population. In most of the advanced countries now production per man engaged in agriculture is increasing at rates between 4 per cent and 6 per cent per year. The figure for Great Britain is 4·1 per cent per year. This is compounded by output increasing at the rate of 2·7 per cent per year, and the number of men at work in agriculture decreasing at 1·4 per cent per year. This 2·7 per cent per year increase in output is far in excess of the rate of increase in British demand, which is only about 1·2 per cent per year (compounded of 0·8 per cent per year increase in population and 0·4 per cent per year increase in consumption per head). A similar situation, with production increasing much faster than demand, prevails in all the advanced countries, except the United States, Norway, and Sweden, where agricultural production has been deliberately kept down by government action.

It will be remembered that we have defined the subsistence minimum as approximately 250 kg. of grain-equivalent per person per year. In North America and Western Europe direct consumption of grain is under 100 kg. per person per year. But the grain equivalent of all the meat, dairy produce, fruit, etc. which we consume, together with our textile fibres, tobacco, alcoholic drinks, etc., brings the grain equivalent of our consumption up to about 2 tons per person per year. This is not of course a physical quantity of grain, but it does represent a demand on agricultural resources, on labour, land, fertilisers, etc., which would otherwise have been capable of producing this quantity of grain. So, in quite a real sense of the term, we can be said to be living at almost exactly eight times the subsistence level. If each of us reduced his diet to subsistence level, it would set free enough agricultural resources to feed seven other people at the same level.

However, for the present at any rate, let us take such a standard—take that of the United States for convenience—as the rate at which people are to be fed, also to be provided with textile fibres, tobacco and the rest. Let us also take the United States figure, which is representative, for the ratio of family dependants to workers. Having made these definitions we can then show how many complete families can be fed—indeed fed to satiation—by the labours of one man working in agriculture.

Numbers of families* which could be provided with food and all other agricultural requirements (at present-day US consumption standard) by one man working in agriculture.

	1934–8	1950–1	1959–60	Rate of increase % per year
Germany		1·7	3·1	5·2
France	2·8	3·3	6·1	6·2
Denmark	3·8	5·9	9·0	5·3
UK	4·2	6·4	9·7	4·1
Canada	4·1	6·8	11·8	5·0
Australia	9·6	11·7	15·7	2·2
US	5·5	10·1	17·6	5·6
New Zealand	16·7	21·2	28·2	4·2

* Families computed from US average of dependants to labour force.

If we are approaching the stage where the work of one man in agriculture can meet the complete requirements of some thirty families, it naturally follows that under such circumstances a country need only employ about 3 per cent of its labour force in agriculture; and indeed, if it tries to keep agricultural employment higher, it will suffer an embarrassing surplus. Furthermore if productivity per man goes on increasing at the rate of some 5 per cent per year, as it shows every sign of doing, even this low proportion of agricultural workers in the labour force will have to show a rapid continued further reduction.

It is true that these extraordinary advances have only been made by use of large inputs of equipment, fertiliser, transport and other non-agricultural products. It is sometimes contended that these low proportions of the labour force required in agriculture in modern communities are illusory in the sense that every farmer has a large number of industrial workers standing behind him to provide these needs. But even the amount of industrial employment required to meet them is much less than is supposed. The production of agricultural equipment, fertilisers, etc., has also been highly mechanised, and great improvements in efficiency have been made in these fields too. A careful calculation by Dovring showed that the amount of such "indirect employment" in American agriculture, expressed as a percentage of agricultural employment, has been rising, but even now only represents about 43 per cent of the numbers in agricultural employment.

7

The Possibilities of Irrigation

IT IS obvious that plants need water, and that nothing will grow in the rainless desert. The story that a new plant had been bred in Israel which was able to condense water out of the atmosphere, to provide not only for its own needs but also for those of adjacent plants, was a piece of third-rate science fiction, promulgated by some scientific journalist who should have known better.

In the physiology of plant growth water has innumerable functions to perform. However, the quantities of water used up in these processes are very small. The main demand of the plant for water is for transpiration, that is for evaporation from its leaves and stem. At one time it was thought that each plant had a "transpiration ratio", i.e. consumed a given quantity of water for each unit of crop. This idea is now known to be erroneous. In cold weather there is little evaporation; but at the same time the plant is not making much growth. The majority of plants make no growth at all when the temperature is below 5 degrees Centigrade (41° F.), and do not produce substantial amounts of carbohydrate until the temperature has reached 10° C. (50° F.). At these and higher temperatures considerable evaporation is taking place. It takes place through the open stomata (literally "mouths"), or microscopic openings on the leaf surface. If they were not open, the leaf would not be able to take in carbon dioxide to continue the process of photosynthesis, and even if we can contemplate without demur the cessation of growth of the plant, the prevention of evaporation by the closing of the stomata, at any rate for more than a limited period, would cause the plant to become

uncomfortably hot. Most living things keep themselves cool by evaporation, including our own
mechanism for sweating on a hot day. Physiologists
cannot quite agree on what is the maximum
temperature which plant tissues can stand, but it is
somewhere in the 30s (degrees centigrade). There
are a few anomalous plants such as cacti, which
have very thick skins, enabling them to withstand
high temperatures, but they are not of agricultural
importance. Even though the atmospheric temperature may be well below 30° C., the radiation from
the sun falling directly on the leaves of a plant
throughout a hot day would raise its temperature far
higher.

It was only comparatively recently that Dr
Penman, F.R.S., Director of the Soil Physics branch of
Rothamsted Agricultural Experiment Station, showed
that the greater part of the water demand of plants
arose simply out of this necessity of evaporating
enough to keep themselves cool. It is true that some
recent experimental work, particularly in Australia,
has shown that it is possible temporarily to close the
stomata by means of chemical sprays, and that the
plant's water consumption is thereby immediately reduced. In other words, a plant with its stomata open
on a hot day may be cooling itself a little more than
is physiologically necessary, and using up additional
water in the process. But the amount of water so in-
volved does not seem to be significant compared with
the main requirement for evaporation. The Australian experiments may develop a treatment which will
be useful for helping plants to meet short spells of
exceptionally hot weather. But even so, it will be at

the sacrifice of the rate at which they can produce carbohydrates.

One would have thought that it was a fairly simple problem in physics, but it is in fact most difficult for a physicist to prepare a formula showing the amount of evaporation to be expected under varying circumstances. Thornthwaite[1] devised a simplified system for predicting what he called "evapo-transpiration" (i.e. the amount of transpiration from the leaves and stems of plants, plus the evaporation from any vacant ground between them) taking into account temperature, length of day, and latitude. Even so, the results are still approximate. Further factors which should be taken into account are the winds, some of which bring and some of which carry away moisture or heat, and the nature of the vegetation. However, insofar as the quantity of incoming solar heat on to any piece of land is known, the physicist can then proceed to draw up a "thermal balance sheet". Winds may contribute to either side of the balance sheet, but generally cannot be predicted. Some plants, with glossy leaves—often found in the tropics—possess the useful attribute of being able directly to reflect back anything up to a quarter of the incoming solar radiation. If water is available, it will be evaporated or transpired by plants, and the evaporation of each gram of water uses up a substantial amount of heat. Even if evaporation is taking place, very much more so if it is not, the balance of the heat not neutralised by evaporation will be stored in the soil, to be radiated back into the atmosphere at night. The temperature of the soil (and of

[1] *Geographical Review*, January 1948.

the plants growing on it) can only be allowed to rise to a limited degree, if the plants are to flourish. It follows that a predictable amount of water has to be evaporated, which can be calculated from the amount of incoming solar radiation, with allowance for a few other factors, such as the reflectivity of the leaves, conversely of their roughness (which may cause them to absorb further heat from the wind), of the extent to which a rise in soil or plant temperatures is permissible, and also of the extent of uncovered soil between the plants. (It is safe to allow this latter to rise to a higher temperature than the plants themselves.)

Subject to the above qualifications, we reach the interesting conclusion that, in a given climate, and for a given length of the crop-growing period, all plants should use approximately the same amount of water—a conclusion very different from that which irrigation engineers and administrators had previously believed.

Besides the amount of water required, the frequency of its application is also an important question. All plants obtain their water through the roots. Trees and bushes have deep roots, and can live for a long while on reserves of water stored in the subsoil, so long as these are replenished in due course, either by rainfall or by irrigation. Lucerne has always been known to be very deeply rooted. It has only fairly recently been discovered that cereal plants will put down very deep roots, at any rate when provoked into doing so by dry weather. Some other crops, however, such as potatoes and tobacco, are incapable of putting down deep roots, and therefore need watering much more frequently. Of all crops the most shallow rooted, and therefore the most likely to be adversely affected by even a temporary water shortage, is grass.

Grass, which is also the most troublesome crop to keep watered, yields the least valuable return per unit of irrigated land. Cereals yield a less valuable return than other crops. The amount of irrigation water which is available for application is bound to be limited, and if all crops, for each day of the growing season, use approximately the same amount of water, then commonsense tells us that we should use our irrigation water on the highest-valued crops —so long as they don't have a much longer growing season than the lower-valued crops. Government policy in India, on the other hand, has been to use as much irrigation water as possible on the cereal crops, on the grounds that the need for them was most urgent. This might be a defensible policy in time of near-famine, but not otherwise. Irrigation water used on crops such as cotton and tobacco, some of whose output might indeed be available for export, would make it possible to buy the same quantity of cereals that the irrigation water might have produced, and still leave a good deal of value to spare.

Another very harmful fallacy has influenced Indian policy on irrigation. It has been said that fertilised plants need more water than unfertilised, and therefore that it is not safe to use increased quantities of fertiliser without providing additional irrigation water first. This idea is the reverse of the truth. It may have been spread as the result of some pot experiments, which appeared to show heavily-leaved plants transpiring more water than sparsely-leaved plants. But the point is that these pot experiments do not reproduce conditions of the field, where the evaporation from one plant helps to cool its neighbour. Field conditions can be reproduced—admittedly with considerably more trouble and expense—by lysimeter tests. In these a large concrete trough is constructed in the middle of the field, refilled with soil, and planted with the same crop as the surrounding field, but in the lysimeter the input and seepage of water can be precisely measured. Under field conditions heavily fertilised crops are found to require no more water than sparse crops. Furthermore, experiments in several countries confirm that a well-fertilised plant is *better* able to withstand temporary water shortage than a badly-fertilised plant. So let the Indian fertiliser programme go ahead with all possible speed. Irrigation is desirable too, but is certainly not a necessary precondition for the application of fertiliser.

Irrigation experts in English-speaking countries cling to their traditional units of gallons, cusecs and acre-feet. But nowhere is the transition to metric units more advantageous than here. In British or American units it is necessary to stop and do a tedious calculation every time you want to relate one to the other. The metric unit for measuring water is a cubic metre (which weighs 1 ton); water supplied to the depth of 1 metre, either by irrigation or by rainfall, over an area of 1 hectare, represents 10,000 cubic metres. So it is very easy to reckon from one unit to another.

To estimate the economic value of water applied

in irrigation is a very complex task. It is not easy to measure the increase in crop yields brought about by irrigation, in comparison with the yields of similar unirrigated land nearby. And after this has been done, it is also necessary to take into account any additional seed, fertiliser, labour, draught animal power, etc. which the farmer may have had to put into his irrigated land. The estimate can only be made by detailed scrutiny of farm accounts, followed by the preparation of a production function, or, better still, a mathematical programme for the use of water under varying circumstances.

One does not associate the idea of farm accounts with India. But it has been possible to persuade Indian farmers, in a few representative areas, to keep precise records of all their incomings and outgoings. Analysis of these accounts shows that the application of 1 cubic metre of water produces, on the average, an additional net yield (after offsetting all additional production expenses) of 0·25 kg. of wheat, or alternatively corresponding quantities of other cereals economically exchangeable for 0·25 kg. of wheat. At world prices, this is worth about 1·8 American cents; though the internal price of cereals in India (at the present dollar-rupee rate of exchange) is about 75 per cent higher.

In the hands of a skilful farmer, a limited supply of irrigation water can yield a much higher net return in the case of maize. A comparatively small quantity of water applied at certain critical periods in the growth of this crop has a very big effect on the final harvest.

But all over the world, the really high net returns

to each cubic metre of water are found, as was to be expected, in growing crops such as potatoes, fruit and vegetables, tobacco, cotton, wine. These are crops which can generally only be grown by skilled and experienced farmers, well supplied with fertilisers and the necessary specialised equipment, and, most important of all, with good transport and access to markets. These conditions are difficult or impossible of fulfilment by the near-subsistence cultivator in India or elsewhere. Supplying irrigation water is very much a matter of "to him that hath shall more be given"—it is most valuable in the hands of farmers already wealthy. Irrigation can play a valuable part in the development of such countries as India. But in their case the provision of roads and access to markets, and fertiliser, should come first.

Much valuable irrigation water is put onto sugar cane, particularly in India. Sugar cane is an unusually demanding crop, because its growing season lasts for almost the whole year. The marginal productivity of irrigation water applied to sugar cane, when sugar is valued at its present world price, is very low. At the high internal prices which some countries (including India) guarantee to their producers, the use of water for this purpose appears remunerative. It has not occurred to such governments that they might in effect be taking water away from what might have been more productive uses.

A sophisticated series of mathematical programmes for the use of water by Californian farmers under various circumstances yields the interesting result that at the same price of about 1.8 cents per cubic metre (which represents the marginal value of water for growing cereals under Indian conditions) there is marked break in the demand function. If the charge for water is above that, they will use water on their land to an average depth of 70 cm. When water is cheaper they will use about twice as much, though even if they got their water for nothing they would not apply it to a depth of more than 155 cm. This latter figure represents the average rate of evaporation in California—a little over 4 mm. per day, averaged over the whole year. If the farmer applied water at more than the maximum evaporation rate, he would soon waterlog his soil. This indeed is what has happened in some areas in India, and still more in Pakistan, where mismanagement has led to the over-application of water to certain lands. Waterlogging, once it has occurred, can only be remedied by expensive drainage channels, or the sinking of deep power-operated tube-wells.

To most people, the idea of irrigation conjures up a vision of big dams, and the bigger the better, so far as some people are concerned—they give the engineers more to do, and the politicians and the journalists more to talk about. But here, more than in any other field of economics, the law of diminishing returns applies. In any country, the number of potential dam sites is limited. The water yield which can be obtained from them varies very widely, and the engineers naturally will pick the most productive sites first. The fact that one big dam has been economically successful is therefore very far from constituting an argument for expecting the next one to be—indeed it may indicate the opposite.

There would be no point in building dams if

rivers flowed evenly throughout the year. The whole idea of a dam is that the river flow is much higher at some seasons than others, and the purpose of the dam is to store the surplus flow for use at other times of the year. This tends to be quite a costly business for each cubic metre of water stored. How much better therefore if nature assists in the storage process. The best way for this to happen is for much of the rainfall on the watershed to fall in the form of snow, which is then "stored" in this form throughout the winter, and furthermore released gradually, and not all at once, as it melts in the following summer. So low-cost irrigation has been possible where use can be made of flooding snow-fed rivers, without the necessity of building large dams, in Pakistan and Northern India, in California, and in the Andes. The Nile is partly snow-fed—everyone knows the paradox about snow on the Equator— there are indeed very high ranges there. But in this case a considerable degree of "storage" is also provided by large lakes, and a remarkably good and even flow of water ensues for four or five months of the year, long enough to grow a crop in the Egyptian climate. The ancient Egyptians were practising irrigation from the natural flow of the Nile thousands of years ago, and it was only at the end of the nine· teenth century that the damming of the Nile was begun (in order to make double-cropping possible).

But to conclude from this experience that large rivers can also be remuneratively dammed in Southern India, South Africa, Brazil, Australia, and other countries with little or no snow-fed storage is a serious mistake.

Large dams are now often designed so as to yield hydro-electric power as well as water. In the case of the high Aswan Dam now being constructed in Egypt, the largest in the world, and some of the large Indian dams, the economic value of the hydro-electric power alone fully offsets the cost of the dam, yielding, in effect, a supply of water free of charge. Other dams already built in India, however, are only yielding water at unduly high cost. In a country so short of capital as India, it is a very grave mistake to waste in this manner capital which is so urgently needed for many other purposes.

It must be remembered also that we need more than water delivered at the dam. It has to be distributed to where it is to be actually used. By designing a very large dam, engineers can effect substantial economies in the amount of concrete construction required per cubic metre of water stored. But the larger dams also require longer distributive systems. Generally speaking, the additional expense of the distributive system outweighs, or more than outweighs, the saving in the cost of building the large dam—especially when, as has happened in India the distributive system is artificially lengthened, for political reasons, to supply unduly distant farmers.

There remain two less glamorous but more economical methods of obtaining irrigation water, namely small dams and wells. Small dams are of course most readily constructed in hilly or undulating country; and wells on river plains. In hilly country it may be necessary to dig a very deep well, often through hard rock, to obtain an uncertain water supply. Even American farmers, with their good low-cost pumping equipment, would consider a well 30 metres deep about at the economic limit of feasibility, unless they were growing some exceptionally high-valued crop.

What is known as the Indo-Gangetic Plain is one of the world's poorest and most densely populated areas. It includes almost the whole of West Pakistan, and a great part of Northern India. Through it flow the Indus and the Ganges with their tributaries. Almost everywhere in this vast area water can be obtained by sinking a well to a depth of about 10 metres. For thousands of years water has been obtained from such wells, laboriously hauled up by men or oxen. But even at low Indian wages, bearing in mind that oxen have to be fed if they are to do heavy work, this operation is pretty well at the limit of economic feasibility. However, the recent introduction of power pumps, whether diesel or electrically driven, has made all the difference. It is now possible to deliver water at a cost which is only a fraction of the estimated additional yield which could be obtained from it. Moreover, this does not require government-operated wells, with their inevitable bureaucracy, delays and high costs. The cost of sinking a well and providing a pump is within the means of many individual farmers. Pakistan has developed these possibilities faster than India by specially relaxing the conditions for importing the materials and equipment required. Such wells however are now spreading rapidly in India also. When the first power pump appears in a village, the farmer who has constructed it charges his neighbours a maximum price for the water, which approaches the net value of the additional crop which they can obtain by using it. At this price he makes a very large profit for himself. Very soon however other farmers install pumps too; and competition between them rapidly drives the price down to something nearer the cost of operating and depreciating the well and the pump.

Once such wells are installed in large numbers, the level of the water table in the sub-soil may fall. The pumps however will be able to deal with depths substantially greater than the present without a serious increase in cost. What will be the outlook in the long run will depend on the speed and manner in which the sub-soil water is replenished, and on this subject, at present, hydrologists are unable to reach any conclusions. They do point out, however, that in this respect there is nothing in the world like the Indus Valley, in which nearly all the population of West Pakistan live. Here we have a bed of alluvium nearly 200 metres deep, saturated with water. It will take a long time to pump that dry.

Irrigation in the past has been mainly applied, and the method will continue to be used in Asia for some time, through channels and furrows. But commercial farmers everywhere are finding that spray irrigation, even though it requires them to pay a good deal more for equipment and labour, makes a much more economical use of the water.

The variability of the flow of rivers, and the problems of designing dams, are such that in most cases engineers think that they have done very well if they manage to conserve as much as 25 per cent of the entire annual flow of the river. It is true that plans are afoot to conserve eventually as much as 70 per cent of the total flow of the Nile; but this is an unusual river, and in any case is having a remarkably large amount spent upon it. Indian engineers have made careful plans which indicate that, even in the distant future, they only expect to capture 21 per cent of the entire flow of Indian rivers. This would about triple the present supply of irrigation water received from the rivers, and enable them eventually to irrigate 31 million hectares. If properly fertilised as well as irrigated, we could look to this land to yield 4 tons of grain per hectare.

We sometimes hear about threats of a world water shortage. To take account of the upward trend of water consumption, we will use the United States official estimate for 1980, which is very considerably in advance of present-day consumption. Domestic water requirements are estimated at 168 cubic metres per person per year—about half a ton, or 100 imperial gallons per person per day, which is quite a lot. However, water consumption requirements by manufacturers—steel works and oil refineries are among the biggest consumers—were as high as 620 cubic metres per head of population per year.

Most of this water supply however is not used up, It is returned to the rivers, in a more or less contaminated state. The amount actually used, i.e. evaporated, is only 22 cubic metres per person per year out of the domestic supply, and 56 cubic metres per person per year out of the industrial supply. We have not yet mentioned power stations, which require huge quantities of water for cooling, with a gross intake estimated for 1980 at 1530 cubic metres per person per year, but a net evaporation of only 9. Power stations do not seriously contaminate their cooling water, although they return it to the rivers hot, which is also bad for fish life.

The figures given for agricultural irrigation, however (the American official estimate is that this will be on a somewhat smaller scale in 1980 than now), were for a gross intake of nearly 1000 cubic metres per year per head of the entire population of the United States and a net evaporation of 620. Agriculture is already far the largest consumer of water, in the sense of evaporating it so that it cannot be used again. Whether returning water to a stream when heated or contaminated counts as "using" it is a matter which may be debated. Domestic and industrial contamination can in fact be completely removed, if we are prepared to spend enough on waste and sewage treatment—though how much this would cost cannot yet be accurately estimated.

The total flow of water in the rivers of the United States is 8000 cubic metres per year per head of the estimated 1980 population. This really should leave a substantial margin to meet all these needs. The United States authorities regard a large part of this stream flow as "required" to dilute the sewage, industrial wastes and power station discharges to the point where they cease to be offensive, or to kill the fish. For 1980 they estimate that 2000 cubic metres per head will be required for this purpose—considerably less than now. It is hoped that sewage treatment will have considerably improved by that time.

The United States water problems arise, of course, from the fact that the stream flow is not evenly distributed, being over-abundant in some regions, and rather scarce throughout the West. When water is really scarce, however, it has been found, e.g. in the construction of a steel plant in Utah, that the industrialist can reduce his water requirement to one-fiftieth of normal gross intake by a system of re-circulation. Power stations can also discharge their outflow into ponds, leave it to cool, then re-circulate it—of course at additional expense.

It so happens that, for the world as a whole, the average river flow is also about 8000 cubic metres per year per head of population—exactly the same as in the United States. This river flow is about one-quarter of the total rainfall which falls on the land, the rest being evaporated before it reaches the streams by vegetation, or from soil, rock, or water surfaces.

Big cities, it is pointed out, find it necessary to go far afield for their water supplies. In doing so they not only spoil the landscape, but also (a factor less frequently pointed out) render themselves extremely vulnerable. In 1941–42 both Hong Kong and Singapore had to surrender as soon as the invaders cut their water supply. Evelyn Waugh made the strange prophecy that Los Angeles would disappear as suddenly as it had grown, and that by the end of the century turkeys would again be nesting in Sunset Boulevard. He made the irrefutable point that, in a time of crisis, a handful of parachutists or partisans could cut its water supply.

Suppose, however, that some city takes note of this warning, and decides instead carefully to "harvest" its own rainfall. (This is probably what our descendants will do, as a matter of course. As things are now, and so long as they are allowed to do so, they find it considerably cheaper to raid somebody else's water.) We may imagine a city laid out as the English new towns are now, i.e. with 220 square metres of space in all per person (i.e. about 11,000 persons per square mile of gross area, if we prefer to think that way). We will also make the generous assumption that two-thirds of the entire space consists of private gardens and public open space, covered with grass or other vegetation. We will assume a normal European rain-fall of 75 cm. (30 inches) and a not unduly hot climate, with the evapo-transpiration from the grass and vegetation averaging 50 cm. per year, or two-thirds of the oncoming rainfall. The remainder will run off into the streams, or sink into the subsoil, from which it can be recovered by wells. This means a water recovery of the full 75 cm. of rainfall from one-third of the area covered by structures and roads, and 25 cm. from the other two-thirds of the area, or 41·7 cm. in all. With 220 square metres area per person, this will give 90 cubic metres of water per person. The estimated United States consumption for 1980 was 80 cubic metres per person net. But two-thirds of this was for industrial purposes, which is estimated to be growing very rapidly. The actual consumption per person in 1954 had been 50 cubic metres net, and we may take this as a standard requirement. We conclude therefore that the proper harvesting of the rainfall actually falling on the city, with the proper cleansing of waste water and sewage, would provide all the city's water requirements, with a considerable margin to spare. Even in a climate of substantially lower rainfall and higher evaporation this would still be the case.

So much for the world's supposed water shortage.

Finally we come to what we now call, with our taste for cumbrous and unnecessary neologisms, the "desalination" of sea water (what is wrong with our existing word "distillation"?). The short answer is that the most ambitious scheme yet projected, using nuclear power on a very large scale, will still not be able to distil water at a cost less than 8 cents per cubic metre—and then there will be very heavy charges for distributing the water on top of that. Undoubtedly there are some densely populated industrial districts, and some other cities not so densely populated, but situated in arid climates, which would be willing to pay this amount, and indeed more. The city of Colorado Springs recently offered to pay as much as 36 cents per cubic metre for water which is at present being offered at an extremely low charge for irrigation, and there is a case on record of one city in Texas, in emergency, paying 70 cents.

We may possibly envisage some time in the distant future, when food prices are far higher than they are now, when farmers would be willing to buy water for irrigation at 8 cents per cubic metre. But no farmer in the world would think of it now, except for growing a few vegetables in some completely arid climate.

8

International Trade in Agricultural Products

WE MUST begin this chapter with further obvious statements. So much of economics consists of statements which are obvious as soon as one comes to look at them, but which for various reasons seem to escape the notice alike of active statesmen and of learned professors.

A country has three reasons for needing to increase agricultural production. The first is to enable its people to be better fed (and clothed) all round, both the farm and the urban population. We have seen how urgent this need is for very poor communities living near to the subsistence line, and how it becomes progressively less urgent with economic advance. In a very poor community, almost the whole population is engaged in agricultural production. If it is to become wealthier, more industrialised and urbanised, a lesser number of agricultural producers must be able to produce enough to satisfy the requirements of the urban population, which often consumes per head more agricultural produce (the composition and quality of the food being taken into account) than the agricultural population itself. The second reason for which a country needs to increase productivity per man engaged in agriculture is to enable a relatively declining agricultural labour force to feed an increasing non-agricultural labour force.

There is a third reason for producing more agricultural produce, a very important one, requiring substantial amounts, which economic planners however nearly always forget. This is the need to obtain more agricultural produce for export. Why do we need to export at all, the planners ask, being generally inward-gazing and insular men, great admirers of the perfection of their own plans. The answer is, of course, to pay for imports. Many economic planners think rather vaguely of imports as something they can do without, replacing them by home production; or that, if they do need them, a kind benefactor will give them all the foreign exchange that they need. How far from the world of reality. Many countries have set out to "replace" imports, some of them, like Australia, well-endowed with capital and skilled labour. Some imports are replaced, and a lot of fuss made about it. But it invariably happens that new import requirements spring up faster than the traditional imports are replaced, and the country ends up by importing more than ever.

The countries which need to import least, in proportion to their national product, are the large countries. The word "large" in this case does not refer to geographical size. Greenland is about the largest country in the world, but has to import everything which it consumes, except fish. What counts principally is size of the national product; and for this purpose it makes no difference whether this is produced by a small population with a high productivity per head, or a large population with a small productivity per head. Diversity of natural resources, availability of oil, minerals and forest products, also makes a difference. But size of national product is the principal determining factor in import requirements. We get the same result whether we are comparing countries of different size, or looking at the course of affairs in one country as time goes on, namely that every time real (i.e. discounted for price changes) national product goes up by 1 per cent, imports have to go up by 0·7 per cent.

This of course is *not* the same thing as saying that seven-tenths of every increase in the national product will be spent on imports. If, at the beginning of the period, a country has a national product of 100 and imports of 30, then if national product rises by 1, imports will rise by 0·21. Even so, this means that over a fifth of the increase in national product will be consumed in the form of imports.

Relatively, however, imports are always rising more slowly than national product. This means that, with a very large economy like the present day United States, imports can fall to only 5 per cent of national product. India is also a large economy. Though product per head is low, this is largely offset by size of the population. Because of this, India also has a much lower ratio of imports to national product than do the other developing countries.

Being a small country, on the other hand, makes you relatively much more dependent on imports. Even the high-income small countries, such as Switzerland, Belgium and Norway, have a very high ratio of imports to national product. Countries with both a small population and a low income per head, for instance the Central American Republics, are exceptionally dependent on imports.

A government which is sufficiently autocratic can, of course, always decree that its subjects can do without imports. The Tokugawa Regime in Japan, for over two centuries from 1600 to 1868, compelled its people to do without any imports at all, except for the visit of one Dutch ship per year. When Stalin ruled Russia he almost succeeded in reducing imports to nothing. Russia is a very large country, and the harm done was less than it would have been in a smaller economy. But neither of these regimes may be taken as an example of economic efficiency, any more than they were of political justice.

The facts about the need for imports should be clear. There must be some imports of basic raw materials and fuels which the country cannot produce. Many of the developing countries, surprising though it may seem, cannot produce their own food, or at any rate produce it in sufficient variety. And, however strenuous the efforts to replace imported manufactures by the products of home industry, these new industries turn out to have considerable requirements for imported components, and also for imported machinery of all kinds. In a number of cases, where local industry has been over-protected, it has been found that the ensuing imports of components and machinery actually exceed in value the former imports of finished products, which they were intended to replace.

So the "developing" countries are face to face with the question of how to pay for their imports. (There was a time when we simply called them "poor" countries; but in the present sensitive state of international relations that will not do at all. Nor was the proposed title "under-developed countries" well received. Finally, United Nations diplomats hit upon the phrases "developing" and "developed" countries; and these euphemisms are considered tolerable.) What about foreign aid? The amount of this is limited, and the claimants numerous. To do well in foreign aid receipts, per head of your population, you must have a strategic military position—Afghanistan, Jordan and Libya and a few similar countries lead the per head list of foreign aid receipts. Next after them come the French-speaking countries in Africa; and France heads the list of donor countries in the ratio of benefactions to her own national product. While there is a political element in this action, its generosity should not be under-estimated. However, like all forms of generosity, it may sometimes be questioned on the ground that, if it goes too far, it encourages financial irresponsibility on the part of the recipients.

If you are not one of these fortunate few countries, the next best thing to do is to discover oil. But however hard you try, this is not to be had for the asking. The countries in which oil has been discovered generally earn so much from their oil exports that they do not bother much about agriculture, and in some cases are actually letting agricultural production decline. Most of the oil discoveries of recent decades have been in poor or "developing" countries. To ask why this should happen is rather like the old farmer's joke about the visitor who asked why he always put the gate in the muddiest part of the field; the wealthier countries had engaged in a fairly thorough oil search earlier.

Oil is of course an extreme case. But there are many other minerals which are saleable on the world market, and in some cases developing countries find themselves possessed of them. From the point of view of analysing the economic needs of a developing country, it is permissible to class oil, and all other saleable minerals, as "food substitutes". They can contribute to paying for imports, and in that way release agricultural produce which otherwise would have had to be exported for this purpose. If sufficiently abundant, they can even be exchanged in the world market for imported food. What applies to minerals also applies to forestry or fishery products, if the country possesses them in exportable quantities.

Besides the cases of oil-rich countries like Iraq and Libya, which in consequence have neglected their agriculture, we get a number of other cases, some of them rather surprising, of developing countries which have to import food. In India's case, both American suppliers and Indian recipients think of the imported grain as a measure to meet a temporary emergency, and look forward to the time when India can at least supply her own grain. But then there are cases like Ceylon, whose agriculture is specialised for export production of tea, rubber and copra, and which imports a large proportion of her food supplies. A number of other developing countries are in a similar, though not so extreme, situation. In Africa there are certain regions with a substantial export income from minerals or plantation crops, which have to import food, even though other regions within their own countries are substantial agricultural producers, because internal transport is too difficult.

The final form of "food substitute" for a developing country is, of course, when it can itself become an exporter of industrial products. Japan, which had a large and growing population with very limited agricultural resources, entered this field as early as the 1880s. A number of the developing countries are now doing so, as we shall see below.

But subject to the above qualifications, it is the developing countries which, poor though they may be, have to *export* agricultural produce. Even if their own people are hungry, there is no alternative, because their need for various imports is so urgent, and because foreign aid is so limited.

Now comes their grievance, which is quite genuine. We are increasing our exports of agricultural produce, they say, and all the time we find that each unit of agricultural produce which we export is worth less and less, in terms of the quantity of imported manufactures which it will buy.

The situation is set out in full in the table on pages 136–7.

"Raw materials" include substantial quantities of agricultural products (textile fibres) but also minerals other than oils and fuels, and forest products. Unfortunately it is impossible to distinguish them, and food and raw materials have to be grouped together for the purposes of this table. Fuels, however, can be shown separately—this trade now consists principally of oil.

The first thing which one will notice from the table is the high proportion of the imports of the developing countries which consist of food, raw materials and fuel—about a third, though the proportion is diminishing.

The next two columns show the course of prices, indicating all too clearly how world prices of manufactures have risen, while the prices of food and raw materials exported from the developing countries have fallen. These trends continued into 1967, with the index for manufactures rising to 107 and for food and raw materials falling to 100. The exporting countries had to sell 32 per cent more primary produce to buy the same quantities of manufactures in 1967 as in 1955. Those who wish to make a still stronger case can point out that if we compare 1967 with 1950 the proportion becomes 53 per cent. However, it is agreed that about 1950–51 the prices of food and raw materials were exceptionally high. The comparison with the year 1955, which was a representative year of its period, leads to a conclusion which is serious enough.

The next two columns will surprise us. We tend to think of food and raw materials as coming from the developing countries, but in fact of all international trade in these commodities, the developed countries provided 57 per cent in 1955 and 62·4 per cent in 1966.

So the developed countries, at the beginning of the period already holding a large share in the world export market for food and raw materials, are now yet more strongly competing in it. One thinks first, naturally, of exports from the United States, Canada, Australia, New Zealand and South Africa. These however constituted only about half of the food and raw materials exports from the developed countries, both in 1955 and in 1966. The other half came—though it is hard to believe—from Western Europe. We must not forget Danish butter, French wine, Italian and Spanish fruit, Scandinavian timber.

The size of the world market for food and raw materials—measured in quantity not in money—is seen to have been rising 4·4 per cent per year. On the face of it, this is quite a satisfactory rate, and it

| | International trade of developing countries $ billion at current prices | | | | | | Prices (1963 base) | |
| | FOOD & RAW MATERIALS (not fuels) | | FUELS | | MANUFACTURES | | Manufactured exports | Food & raw materials (not fuels) exported from developing countries |
	Exports	Imports	Exports	Imports	Exports	Imports		
1955	14·64	5·42	5·90	2·73	3·03	13·78	91	112
1956	15·01	5·75	6·43	2·91	3·29	15·59	95	111
1957	15·09	6·29	7·00	3·14	3·18	17·97	98	114
1958	14·40	5·97	7·43	3·00	2·78	16·99	97	109
1959	15·01	6·14	7·36	2·85	3·24	16·57	96	103
1960	15·71	6·80	7·65	2·90	3·84	18·30	98	102
1961	15·38	6·72	8·10	3·00	3·98	19·10	99	98
1962	15·75	6·96	8·87	3·11	4·26	19·20	99	96
1963	17·03	7·55	9·48	3·02	4·86	20·44	100	100
1964	18·17	8·38	10·63	3·12	5·65	22·54	101	103
1965	18·57	8·45	11·31	3·25	6·39	24·81	103	102
1966	19·17	9·13	12·22	3·44	7·37	26·87	106	102

Quantities measured at prices of 1963 $ billion

	World total exports of food & raw materials (not fuels)			Manufactured imports purchaseable by exports of developing countries		Imports of developing countries other than those paid for by fuel exports[b]	
	Developing countries	Developed countries	Total	Food & raw materials (not fuels)	Total[a] including manufactured exports	Food, raw materials & fuels	Total
1955	13·1	17·5	30·6	16·1	19·4	6·8	16·9
1956	13·5	19·0	32·5	15·8	19·3	6·8	18·2
1957	13·2	20·2	33·4	15·4	18·6	7·4	20·4
1958	13·2	19·7	32·9	14·8	17·7	7·3	19·1
1959	14·6	21·6	36·2	15·6	19·0	7·3	19·0
1960	15·4	24·1	39·5	16·0	19·9	8·0	20·9
1961	15·7	25·0	40·7	15·5	19·5	7·9	21·1
1962	16·4	25·6	42·0	15·9	20·2	8·0	20·9
1963	17·0	27·1	44·1	17·0	21·9	8·0	21·5
1964	17·6	29·3	46·9	18·0	23·6	8·3	23·0
1965	18·2	29·8	48·0	18·0	24·2	8·4	24·2
1966	18·8	31·2	50·0	18·1	25·0	8·8	25·6
% per year average rate of growth	3·1	3·1	4·4	2·1	3·4	1·4	3·6

[a] Assuming that world export price index for manufactures is applicable both to developing and to developed countries.

[b] Assuming that spending of earnings from fuel exports is distributed between food and raw materials and manufactured imports in the same proportion as the total imports of developing countries under these heads.

is certainly wrong to talk about it as a contracting market. However, after we have allowed for increasing competition from the developed countries, the market for food and raw materials exported from the developing countries is expanding at the rate of only 3·1 per cent per year.

In the next column we take account of the deteriorating terms of trade, that is to say, of the quantity of manufactures purchaseable by the developing countries in return for given quantities of their exports of food and raw materials. By the time we have taken this into account, the rate of growth is seen to be only 2·1 per cent per year, which is unsatisfactory.

However the next column is more encouraging. The developing countries, driven by obvious incentives, are themselves entering the field of manufactured exports. Starting at only 3 billion dollars in 1955, this figure had been multiplied two and a half fold (at current prices) by 1966. The total capacity of the developing countries to buy manufactured imports, including those they buy in exchange for their own manufactured exports, is seen to be rising 3·4 per cent per year when we take this into account.

Outstanding figures of growth of exports of manufactures from developing countries have been shown by Hong Kong, Singapore, Taiwan and Korea. The two latter have received, in the past, considerable help from the United States; it is the gradual withdrawal of this aid which is making them produce manufactured exports to take its place. The growth of manufactured exports from India and Pakistan, though still small in relation to those countries' import requirements, is nevertheless a substantial element in the world market. Some Latin American countries are also beginning to develop manufactured exports.

The last two columns show what the imports of the developing countries have actually been. The figures have had to be adjusted, because we wished to leave out the oil-bearing countries, whose abundant importations are in danger of arousing the envy of their poorer neighbours. We have to make some assumptions about how the spending of the oil-bearing countries is distributed between food and raw materials on the one hand, and manufactures on the other. We are left with approximate figures of what the developing countries, other than the oil-bearing countries, actually do import. Some 40 per cent of their imports consisted of food, raw materials and fuels in 1955, less than 35 per cent in 1966.

We should not expect the imports actually purchased to be exactly the same as "imports purchaseable". Some imports may have been purchased out of the proceeds of loans or foreign aid; or, conversely, the developing countries may have held some of their export earnings in reserve. Moreover the two columns are not defined in precisely the same manner. The "imports purchaseable" calculation is made on the basis of prices of manufactured goods, whereas, as we have seen, a substantial proportion of the imports were in fact food, raw materials and fuels, whose price has been declining relative to the price of manufactured goods.

However, these two columns show approximately similar figures, both in level and in rate of growth. The imports of the developing countries, measured in quantity, have in fact been rising at the rate of 3·6 per cent per year. In view of what has been said above, namely that a rise of 1 per cent in national product requires a rise of 0·7 per cent in imports, this rate of increase of imports will suffice to support a rate of increase of national products of 5·1 per cent per year. (This, it must be remembered, excludes the oil-bearing countries, where national products can and do rise very much faster.) A rate of growth of national products at 5 per cent per year (population in most of these countries is growing at rates between 2 and 3 per cent per year) is really not to be complained about, though of course anything which can be done further to accelerate it should be welcome. Amongst other things which would have to be done comes provision for further export sales, to pay for more imports.

The quantity of exports of food and raw materials from the developing countries, as we have seen above, has been rising at the rate of 3·1 per cent per year. If we take net exports, that is to say less their imports of food and raw materials, other than those paid for by oil exports, we come out with the same result, an average rate of increase of 3·1 per cent per year.

At this point may be mentioned some tentative calculations made in 1963, about the rate at which these countries' net exports of food and raw materials would have to expand[1] during the 1960s, under certain assumptions. These calculations were *not* based

[1] Published in *The Economics of Subsistence Agriculture*, Chapter 10. These calculations refer to a smaller number of "developing" countries than do the United Nations, who include the whole of Latin America and Eastern Europe in this category.

on the amount required to pay for expected import requirements, but simply on the surplus of agricultural products expected to be available for export disposal on various assumptions about the rate at which agricultural productivity could be increased, and also of the income elasticity of demand for food in their own markets, that is to say, how much of their increased output they might be expected to eat themselves. It will be remembered that this figure is very variable, and among some agricultural communities, as in Japan, it is very low.

The first consideration which has to be borne in mind is that a substantial rise in the productivity per head of those engaged in agriculture will of itself make possible, and indeed will almost necessarily lead to, an increase in the proportion of the labour force engaged in non-agricultural activities—only through increased agricultural productivity can they be fed. It might be better to state this proposition the other way round, namely the check to the expansion of industrial employment in many of the developing countries has been simply shortage of food. High food prices in the cities quickly drive the poorer wage-earners back to the agricultural villages. The relationship (which is a semi-logarithmic function) between productivity per person engaged in agriculture, and the proportion of the labour force engaged in non-agricultural employment, can be fairly precisely traced.[2]

The increased productivity of agriculture which will suffice to create new urban employment will also

[2] See *The Economics of Subsistence Agriculture*, Chapter 12.

create a surplus of agricultural produce available for export. The *minimum* conditions for expected increase in exportable supplies of agricultural produce from the developing countries, namely that agricultural productivity should be growing slowly (1 per cent per year) and at the same time that income elasticity of demand for food in the developing countries should be high (0·7) will require a rate of growth of net exports (i.e. after deducting imports) of food and raw materials from the developing countries at the rate of 3 per cent per year. If the rate of productivity growth increases further, as we all hope it will, and if at the same time, the developing countries' internal consumption of agricultural products grows less rapidly, as may well happen, there will be a most acute problem of disposal of agricultural surpluses in the export markets.

The problem stems back to the large share of the available world markets for agricultural products supplied by the developed countries. If the wealthy countries exported less agricultural produce, the poorer countries would find it much easier to earn export revenue, and the terms of trade would move in their favour (i.e. the world prices of agricultural produce, in comparison with the prices of manufactures, would go up).

In the United States, the principal agricultural exporter among the developed countries, the Government already restricts the acreage of a number of principal agricultural products. It will not be easy to ask for further restrictions. Australia and New Zealand are almost entirely independent on agricultural products for their export revenue, and will remain so for a long time to come. If a farmer, in any of these developed countries, can produce agricultural products at a cost which enables him to sell in the present world market, it is rather difficult to justify any Government or international authority in attempting to prevent him from doing so. On the other hand (and this qualification applies, in varying degrees, to all the countries concerned), where he is assisted by some measure of subsidy, or supported price in the internal market, then it does become fair to say that his exportation is, in some degree, subsidised. If the wealthy developed countries are genuinely concerned about the future economic growth of the poorer countries, they should remove all subsidies and price supports from their own agriculture, and then let it find a level at which it can compete at world prices.

In the distant future, what are now the developing countries may be very large exporters of industrial produce, and buyers of agricultural produce from what are now the developed countries. But we should not frame our plans now on a state of affairs which can only come about, at the earliest, twenty or thirty years hence.

9

Modern Standards of Productivity

WE HAVE seen that subsistence requirements, in the true sense of the physiological minimum, are about one-quarter of a ton of grain equivalent per person per year. At the same time actual consumption in North America or Western Europe is about eight times that amount. Medical opinion seems to be fairly clear that most of us would be better off if we ate less. Nevertheless we have taken current United States levels of consumption as a standard in Chapter 6 when estimating how little labour is now required to produce an abundant diet. We now turn to the question of the amount of land to produce, for one person, such abundant feeding. (See table, pages 146–7.)

In the first column we give actual US consumption in 1961–2. The second column gives the wheat equivalents of this consumption, adding up, as is seen, to nearly 2 tons per person. Sugar and edible oils are not themselves the original agricultural products, and in the third column are given the equivalent quantities of sugar cane and groundnut (in shell), the latter being taken as a representative source of oil. The production of 28 kg. of oil however leads to the production as a by-product of some 40 kg. of groundnut cake or meal, whose value per ton (because of its high protein content) is about twice that of maize. This is taken as an offset against other maize requirements.

The entry for maize itself is not for direct human consumption, but for animal feeding stuffs required to provide indirectly for human consumption.

Our diet includes a good deal of meat, and we are accustomed to think of this as coming from grazing animals, requiring considerable areas to produce the supply which we want. But this is progressively ceasing to be the case. A substantial proportion of our meat supply is not produced from grazing at all, but from pig and poultry meat, obtained by feeding grain and other concentrated foodstuffs to animals kept on a very limited area of land indeed. This is also increasingly true about beef. Not many cattle are fed throughout their lives on grain (to produce so-called barley beef); but in the United States a great many cattle, although originally reared on grassland, do all their fattening through grain feeding. It is assumed that in the future two-thirds of all the meat consumption will be in this form.

On present-day standards of feeding by good farmers (and the poor farmers are very quickly being squeezed out of the pig and poultry trades, which have become extremely competitive) 1 kg. of pig meat, deadweight, corresponds to 1·3 kg. of live pig, to produce which 5·3 kg. of cereals are required. A kilogram of poultry meat deadweight, corresponding to 1·5 kg. liveweight, will require only 3·7 kg. of feed. This is raised to 4 to allow for the value of protein supplements, and the average feeding requirement for grain-fed meats is taken at 4·65 kg. maize equivalent per kg. of deadweight meat produced.

Methods of fattening cattle are improving, and it is now estimated that 4·5 kg. of barley are required to yield 1 kg. of liveweight gain.[1]

For grass-fed meats the standard of 1 ton of liveweight per hectare per year (deadweight being only a little over half liveweight in the case of cattle and

[1] Rutherford, *Agriculture*, July 1963.

Kilograms per person per year

	USA consumption 1961–2	Wheat equivalent[c]	Expressed as original agricultural product	Feeding-stuffs Requirement	Maximum yields tons per hectare per year	Land required to provide for one person (square metres)
Wheat	97	97			4·4	220
Fish	5	18				
Meat: grain fed[a]	52	405		241[g]		520
Meat: grass fed	26	202			1·0[l]	285
Milk[b]	299	365	663[e]		10·5	16
Potatoes	49	24			30·3	16
Sugar	49	93			42·7[e]	155
Fruit & vegetables	184	228			100	18
Eggs	18	123		72		
Fats and oils (not butter)	28	108	106[f]		2·5[f]	885
Coffee, tea, cocoa	8	85		80[h]	5·0	16
Grain for brewing and distilling	16	9			4·0[k]	40
Cotton (lint)	10	98			1·2	83
Wool (scoured)	1	31				
Tobacco	3	60			2·9	10
Maize[d]				233[i]	8·8	265
TOTAL		1946				2513

a Assumed that in the future meat consumption will be as in 1961–2 but that ⅔ of it will be grain-fed, i.e. pig meat, poultry meat, grain-finished cattle.

b All dairy products entered at their milk equivalent. Some skim milk and they are thus released for live-stock feeding, which have not been taken into account in the calculation.

c At relative prices prevailing in U.S.A.

d Requirements of grain for feedingstuffs, which may be presented as maize requirements.

e Sugar beet.

f Groundnuts in shell.

g Assumed half pig meat and half poultry meat. See text.

h Offsetting credit entry.

i Sum of column.

j Sufficient obtained as a by-product for grazing.

k Barley.

l Liveweight.

sheep) is the estimate of the British Grassland Research Station, and also of the Irish Agricultural
Institute, for what can be produced on well-fertilised
carefully managed grassland. This however is still
well below the theoretical maximum. We have seen
that, at any rate in a cold moist climate, and fully
fertilised, grassland can be expected to produce 15
tons per hectare per year of dryweight grass, which
should produce 2 tons per hectare per year liveweight
of beef, instead of the 1 ton taken in the table.

Experiments in Australia have shown that, on
irrigated pasture, yields of wool can be obtained at
the rate of 250 kg. per hectare per year (scoured
weight), as well as substantial quantities of mutton.
Even larger numbers of sheep can be fed on a limited
area, but considerable difficulties of parasite control
ensue.

The milk yield per cow is taken at 4·6 tons
per year, a figure which has been obtained in
experiments, and which is only a little above the
national average for the Netherlands. It is assumed
that the cow is fed entirely on grass, hay and silage.

It has been estimated that with a heavy nitrogen
application of 400 kg. per hectare, sufficient grass
will be obtained on 1 hectare[2] to keep 2½ cows
yielding 11½ tons of milk per year. This estimate of
required land is raised by 10 per cent to allow for the
cost of breeding replacement stock, less a credit for
the meat from old cattle.

The other figures for maximum yields are largely
taken from the Netherlands. The maximum yield of

[2] *Land*, Spring 1966, quoting experiments by Holmes
at Wye College.

rice is found in Spain, at 6·2 tons per hectare unmilled weight; the milled weight would be similar to the yield of wheat. For the new strain of rice, IR8, bred at a privately-financed genetic research institute at Los Baños in the Philippines, extravagant claims have been made. In this case, however, they turn out to be true. With adequate water and fertiliser this rice yields under Asian conditions 8 tons per hectare unmilled weight, and its use is now spreading extremely fast.

Regarding sugar, it may be remarked that, if we took sugar cane instead of beet, the maximum yield is obtained in Hawaii, at 222 tons, or almost exactly five times the maximum yield from sugar beet, with approximately similar sugar content. This justifies, as do the figures from grass yield, treating high-rainfall tropical land as the equivalent of at least 5 times the equivalent area of temperate land.

For fruits and vegetables, other than potatoes, a very approximate estimate has to be made. In the Netherlands yields of onions are 30 tons to the hectare, and of tomatoes as high as 90 tons. The average is brought down by fruit.

The estimates for coffee, tea and cocoa are also very approximate. The high figure for cotton is from Israel, for tobacco from Belgium, and for groundnuts from Turkey.

For maize the highest recorded figure is for Canada, at 5·1 tons to the hectare. However, use is made of a formula calculated by Heady[3] of the yield of maize obtained in experiments, when both nitrogen and phosphorous are applied at optimum rates (445 and 377 kg. per hectare respectively).

[3] *Econometrica*, April 1957.

It is seen that methods already in use by good farmers would produce one person's entire requirements for agricultural produce, including textile fibres and minor requirements, by the cultivation of 2513 sq. metres, or a little over a quarter of a hectare (⅔ acre).

Account must also be taken of our need for space to produce our wood and forest products. Other than wood itself, our princial requirement is for wood pulp to make our paper and cardboard. A certain amount of wood is still used as fuel in some places, usually wood which would be of little value for other purposes; but in any case this practice will soon become obsolete, as more economical fuels become available.

It is customary to measure wood "in the round" (foresters and timber merchants have tables to shorten the awkward mathematics of estimating the number of cubic metres in trees of gradually diminishing thickness). With old methods of sawing, 1 cubic metre of wood in the round would yield only about 0·4 cubic metres of useful timber. But some ingenious new methods of using smaller wood have been discovered, and the ratio is now nearer to 0·6. When wood is pulped, of course, the whole bulk in the round is usable.

In economically advanced countries wood consumption per head per year, in the round, is as high as 2 cubic metres in the United States and Canada, and as low as ½ cubic metre in Netherlands, and a few other countries which have to import almost all their timber supplies. In the United States and Canada many houses are still built of wood, and paper is lavishly used. Netherlands standards of consumption should be quite satisfactory, if we are considering a world which is aiming at economical use of land. One of the principal requirements of wood is, of course, for building houses. Comparatively high prices in recent years have caused architects and builders to find many ways of economising on wood, e.g. metal window frames, concrete lintels, use of plywood instead of solid wood, etc. A study by FAO and the Economic Commission for Europe showed that during quite a short period in the 1950s the amount of wood used in a representative European house fell from 9·1 to 7·6 cubic metres. If the house will house four people, and will not have to be replaced for seventy years or more, it is clear that our average per head consumption of wood for building purposes is small.

Waste paper can be re-pulped. It does not make good paper, but is adequate for cardboard. Careful studies in the United States have shown that, with fresh pulp at its present prices, the cost of collecting waste paper, even from places such as offices and hotels where it accumulates, would make the process unremunerative.

No doubt there would be a fearful outcry from newspapers and publishers if it were attempted, but there is a lot to be said for imposing a tax on fresh wood pulp. In the first place it would give more incentive for the collection of waste paper, and might leave our cities and public places tidier. Both newspapers and wrappings might be on a less excessive scale than they are now. It would also give an incentive to perfect processes for obtaining paper from other materials. A process is said to be almost complete for obtaining paper from sugar-cane fibre, of which the world produces very large quantities, at present burned as fuel.

The rate at which forests grow, measured in the round, can be as high as 50 cubic metres per hectare per year in some tropical and sub-tropical areas with good rainfall. In regions in the United States with good temperature and rainfall, such as Northern California and Louisiana, the yield is about 20, as it is in tropical regions with less complete rainfall. In Sweden, on the other hand, which has a big export trade in timber, the yield is only 5·1 cubic metres per hectare per year in the best growing area in the south, and 1·2 in the north.

It seems clear that, as the world comes to organise the supply of its timber requirements more rationally, it will draw much more on the tropics and sub-tropics —not, in most cases, on the indigenous forests, but on planted conifers which have been found to suit the climate (such as *Pinus Taeda* and *Pinus Carribea*). It is true, of course, that the agricultural productivity of Sweden per unit of land, as well as its forest productivity, is lower than that of the tropics. But certainly not in the ratio of 10 to 1.

We have here an interesting illustration of what is called the Economic Law of Comparative Advantage. Though, in absolute terms, Swedish land is less suited both for agriculture and for forestry, nevertheless, of the two alternative uses, it is *relatively* more suited to agriculture. It may be predicted that, as time goes on, relatively more planted forests will appear in the tropics, and relatively more agriculture in the cold climates (except in areas which are too steep or too cold, or where the soil is too thin for agriculture).

Taking as our standard no more than the 20 cubic metres per hectare which can be grown in good United States climates, our requirements of half a cubic metre of wood in the round per head per year can be satisfied by apportioning us 250 sq. metres each.

This means that our combined requirements of agricultural and forest products—at our extravagant standards of consumption, not at subsistence level—can be met by the cultivation or afforestation of just under 2763 sq. metres per person, or 3·62 persons supported by one hectare.

10

The Plenitude of the Earth

THERE STILL persists among some people the extraordinarily erroneous idea that any further additions
to the world's supply of agricultural land must be
very limited. At the World Population Conference in
1954 an eminent geographer, the late Sir Dudley
Stamp, caused some stir by pointing out that the
world was only cultivating about one-third of its
potential agricultural land; and adding that most of
that was cultivated extremely badly. Even so, Sir
Dudley was taking a very cautious view of the possibilities of agriculture in cold climates—a subject on
which further information has become available since
1954.

A survey of the world's potential agricultural land
may be made on the basis of climate.[1] For this purpose, climate is much more important than soil. It is
true that there are certain areas where the soil is
quite exceptionally thin and poor, as on the Pre-
Cambrian Shield in Canada. But apart from these,
most poor soils can be improved out of recognition
by cultivation and fertilisation; and it is assumed that
the world is willing to do this.

Topography and steepness also come into the
question. Really mountainous areas will in any case
have been classified as cold climates. Very steep
slopes, it is true, cannot be cultivated. But they can
make very productive grazing land. Some of the most
steeply sloping land in the world is in New Zealand,
with the world's highest yield of valuable animal
products.

While this method of calculation expects bad soils,

[1] For a full set of maps, see *Population Growth and
Land Use*, pp. 145–8.

where necessary, to be improved, no provision is included, for the present, for mitigating the effects of climate, i.e. by the irrigation of arid or partially arid lands, beyond what has been done already. Nor is any provision made for the artificial heating of tundra, nor for the obtaining of food from the sea, lakes or rivers.

The method used is to define as "standard land" the type of land which is farmed in humid temperate climates, or its equivalent, i.e. land regarded as capable of producing one good crop per year, or a substantial amount of grazing. There are numerous lands whose potential is less than this, because of inadequacies of rainfall, or cold climate. At the same time lands in the humid tropics clearly have a much greater potential. The areas of land subject to these various types of worse or better climates respectively are expressed as their equivalents in "standard land" by means of various coefficients.

The humid tropics are defined as those where temperature is always high and which have rainfall through most of the year. We have seen that, when well fertilised, they are capable of producing grass at no less than five times the rate of the best fertilised temperate land (75 tons dryweight per hectare per year as against 15); also five times as much weight of sugar cane as the best of sugar-beet-producing temperate lands; and two and a half times the quantity of timber. In cropping, it is clear that at least two crops per year can be grown, in some cases three. A general conversion coefficient of 4 is used.

Several alternative classifications of the world's climates have been prepared by geographers. The

system used for this purpose is that proposed by
Thornthwaite.[2] Thornthwaite rightly regards rainfall as the first factor to be looked at in categorising
climate. His classifications are therefore described by
initial letters A to E, ranging from abundant rainfall
to complete aridity. Next he classifies temperature by
dashed letters, ranging from A' for the tropics to E'
for tundra and F' for perpetual frost. A final symbol
is then inserted in the classification in order to show
whether the rainfall is regular (r), summer-deficient
(s), winter-deficient (w), or with the deficiency spread
over the year (d). Thus a C A' (w) climate, typical of
many monsoonal areas, has tropical heat, and rainfall
in the third or "sub-humid" category, with the rainfall deficiency concentrated in the winter months.

In Thornthwaite's classification the region known
as "Taiga" (cold coniferous forest land) covers a
large part of Sweden, Finland, Soviet Russia, Alaska
and Canada. For measurement of agricultural poten-
tiality, this has to be further sub-divided. The method
of analysis used was developed in Finland, where of
course cold climate constitutes the agricultural problem *par excellence*. This method of "accumulated
month-degrees" records average monthly temperatures in degrees Centigrade, and ignores all those of 5
or below—at these temperatures there will be no
growth of crops or grass. For months with average
temperature above this level, however, a point is scored
for each degree Centigrade above 5, and the points
accumulated for the year. It is found that when this
total stands at 38 or higher, all the usual European
crops can be grown, even including sugar beet and

[2] *Geographical Review*, July 1933.

winter wheat (which is more productive than spring-sown wheat). When the figure stands between 30 and 38, spring wheat can be grown, but not sugar beet, and the prospects for peas and beans are dubious. Even turnips become impossible below 23, at which figure the climate is not satisfactory for spring rye, and on the margin for oats, but still satisfactory for winter rye. At 18 it is still possible to grow some kinds of hay, some new strains of barley, and potatoes (which have indeed occasionally been grown in still colder climates). However, land with an accumulated month-degree figure below 18 is treated as valueless for agriculture.

The productivity of irrigated land depends on the temperature, and on the continuity of the water supply. In a tropical climate, e.g. West Pakistan, two crops can be grown, even with incomplete water supplies. It was decided to treat irrigated land as equivalent to 1½ units of standard land.

The co-efficient of one-thirtieth applied to semi-arid land is based on Australian experience. However, the drawing of the boundary of this zone has been conservative. Some areas, e.g. Cyrenaica, included in this zone are in fact capable of some agricultural production.

The population which can be supported at maximum consumption standards is calculated on the basis of 2763 sq. metres required per person for combined agricultural and forestry needs.

The potential agricultural area of the world, it is seen, could provide for the consumption, at these very high standards, of 35·1 billion people, or over 10

Millions of hectares of standard farm land equivalents

Climatic types	Thornthwaite symbols	Equivalent in "standard" farm land	Africa	USA and Canada[a]	Latin America and Caribbean	Western Europe	Eastern Europe[b]	USSR	China	India and Pakistan	Japan, Taiwan and Korea	S E Asia	S W Asia	Australia and New Zealand	Rest Oceania[c]	WORLD
Tropical climate with rainfall sufficient for two or more crops per year	AA'(r) BA'(r) CA'(r)	4	1470	3	1467	—	—	—	—	86	—	926	—	5	117	4074
Wet or humid temperate and sub-tropical climates, tropical climates with irregular rainfall	Rest of A & B	1	151	403	577	140	54	52	99	25	45	191	—	74	28	1839
Sub-humid climates regular rainfall	CB'(r) CC'(r)	5/6	76	74	57	37	65	152	—	—	—	—	—	13	—	474
Sub-humid climates with summer or winter rainfall deficiency	CA'(w) CB'(w) CB'(s) CC'(s)	2/3	540	14	400	27	—	—	66	147	6	15	2	62	—	1279

Category	Köppen code															Total
Sub-humid climates, rainfall deficiency in all seasons	CA'(d) CB'(d) CC'(d)	1/2	57	77	5	—	4	155	53	—	1	—	37	21	—	380
Semi-arid climates suitable for sparse pasture only	D	1/30	21	7	7	1	—	8	6	2	—	—	8	7	—	67
Taiga (cold coniferous forest land) over 38 month degrees		1	—	44	23	29	—	202	42	6	—	—	4	—	—	350
— 30–38 —		9/10	—	175	6	19	—	332	38	6	—	—	3	—	—	579
— 23–30 —	D'	7/10	—	125	4	20	—	153	30	4	—	—	2	—	—	338
— 18–23 —		1/2	—	67	—	8	—	56	21	3	—	—	2	—	—	157
Taiga under 18 month degrees, tundra, perpetual frost, arid land	D'EE'F	0														
Irrigated land		1½	7	17	12	3	—	5	60	53	9	5	17	2	—	190
TOTAL			2292	1006	2558	284	123	1115	415	332	61	1137	75	184	145	9727
Population which could be supported at maximum consumption standards, in billions			8·3	3·6	9·3	1·0	0·4	4·0	1·5	1·2	0·2	4·1	0·3	0·7	0·5	35·1

a Including Alaska and Hawaii.
b Albania, Bulgaria, Czechoslovakia, E. Germany, Greece, Hungary, Poland, Rumania, Yugoslavia.
c Includes New Guinea and islands further east.

times the world's present population. This, it will be remembered, is on the assumption of the general use of agricultural methods already practised by the average farmer in the Netherlands or similar countries, without allowing for any further improvements in agricultural technology, for any provision of food from the sea, or for any extension of present systems of irrigation.

The territory of the United States together with Canada, or of Soviet Russia, could each of them make provision for the whole of the world's present population. Latin America, or Africa, could each make provision for very much more than the whole of the world's present population.

11

Science Fiction Come True

THE ISSUES raised by science-fiction writers have a way of catching up with us. Until recently, long-distance weight-carrying rockets were strictly a science-fiction concept. In 1944 they became deadly weapons of war, in 1957 unmanned satellites, in 1961 man-bearing satellites, and now they carry men to the moon. One really has some grounds for doubting if the imagination of science-fiction writers in the future will be able to keep pace with the development of actual events.

It is not our business at present to enquire either into the incentives, or into the cost; but it appears that there will shortly be not merely visits, but one or more permanent settlements on the moon. This promptly raises the question of food supply—it may of course be necessary to supply the settlements with fresh water and oxygen too, but there are some hopes that these may be obtained by applying intense heat to the rocks. Any possibility of obtaining food will have to be tried, if there is any truth in the estimate by one eminent authority that the transport cost of supplying such a settlement will be of the order of 10 million dollars per gram. The question of food supply has been already seriously investigated by a distinguished international committee of biologists, and I am grateful to Dr Pirie, of Rothamsted, for some interesting information on this subject.

Photographs already available, transmitted by cameras standing on the lunar surface, indicate that it is covered with rock fragments of a sort which could quickly be transformed into productive soil, after an initial admixture of water, mineral nutrients and organic fibres. Supplies of carbon dioxide would soon build up from the exhalations of the settlers and indeed, even if it produced no food, some horticulture would be desirable just for the purpose of reducing the carbon dioxide and restoring oxygen in the atmosphere of the settlement. It would of course be necessary to dilute both the carbon dioxide and the oxygen. Nitrogen, which serves to perform the dilution for us, would be a somewhat cumbrous object to take in the requisite quantities, and it is possible that this function could be performed by helium, which is very much lighter.

So lunar horticulture would begin under an airtight plastic cover. The lunar sunlight lasts continuously for periods of 14 days at a time. There are a number of quick-growing small leafy plants, which could indeed have been germinated in the last days of the preceding lunar night, so as to be ready to start growing as soon as the sunlight arrived, which would yield quite an abundance of leaf by the end of the 14 days of uninterrupted sunlight. A fairly simple apparatus would extract from these leaves and stems substantial quantities of nutritive proteins. There would be left a residue containing some sugars unfit for human consumption, and fibres. At first these would be used for building up the organic content of the soil and, in so far as they were in surplus for this purpose, would be converted by soil micro-organisms back into atmospheric carbon dioxide. However, it should be comparatively simple to devise chemical methods for separating the cellulose from the other substances present, and hydrolysing it to edible starches or sugars.

Looking a little further ahead, we contemplate space

settlements, not necessarily on the surfaces of other planets, which may be inconveniently hot or inconveniently cold, but on large artificial satellites.

Here we may quote an interesting writing (dating from 1958, and showing considerable prophetic power) by J. D. Bernal, the Marxian scientist, who has interesting ideas on a number of subjects:

"It may be asked why anyone should want there to be so many people in the universe. The simple answer in any reasonable world is that people are born because their parents wanted children, and that children as they grow up like each other. If we do not like children enough to bring them into the world when there is any choice in the matter, then the human race would die out, and perhaps would deserve to.

Nor would people be limited to our present earth. It may be several decades, it is unlikely to be more, before seriously organised space-travel occurs. How many people want to live in the perpetual sunshine of outer space is a question for them to settle. Many of the adventurous ones would want to do so already."[1]

In all these cases, whether on a large residential satellite which our descendants might decide to construct, or on the moon, or back on earth, the important question is the rate at which photosynthesis can occur. Plants contain very varying amounts of water, and the usual measure therefore is the photosynthesis of dry matter by weight, measured in grams per day per square metre of area exposed to sunlight.

Some plants have exceptionally high rates of photosynthesis—and are very troublesome weeds. Even in

[1] World Without War, pp. 276-7.

the English climate, which is comparatively unfavourable—the proportion of the solar radiation usable by the plant is considerably higher in the tropics than in temperate climates—the weed *Agrostemma Githago* (corncockle) has been observed growing in warm weather at a rate of 57 grams dryweight per square metre per day (more than half a ton dryweight per hectare *per day*). Water hyacinth, a very troublesome weed in the tropics and sub-tropics, has been observed growing at a rate of 49 (in the same units). Potatoes, if we include the dry matter in their stems and leaves, can grow at a comparable rate. Rates like this for cereals have been claimed, when grown under laboratory conditions, but disputed. There is clear evidence, however, that broccoli and raddish—two favourite plants for the amateur gardener—will grow at the rate of 40–45, under optimum conditions of watering, fertilising and sunlight. Sugar beet will give a figure of 31, and sugar cane figures varying from 30 to 70 under different conditions. A growth of 68 has been estimated for maize.

It has been remarked that science-fiction writers are very wide of the mark if they make their space travellers subsist on pills or potions of some kind, in place of the large bulk of carbohydrate which is our inexorable daily need. A time may come when we are able to organise photosynthesis on an industrial scale ourselves, and use a larger proportion of the solar radiation than plants do. But in view of the extreme complexity of the process of photosynthesis, it is wise not to assume this, and to make our plans on the basis of our continuing dependence upon plant photosynthesis. These figures of maximum rates of plant photosynthesis per square metre per day therefore take on a critical importance. In the average plant, about half the dryweight will consist of material indigestible by us (this, however, includes the proteins in the leaves, indigestible in crude form, which can nevertheless be extracted and used if we wish). If processes can be designed for hydrolysing the fibre, we might be able to use nearly the whole weight; a safer assumption is that we can only use half the weight. Unless we are dealing with root crops, we assume that the plants we grow will provide an adequate amount of protein with the carbohydrate.

Others besides science-fiction writers have had a good deal to say about growing algae for food. Algae were seriously considered as long ago as 1954[2] as a method, not for providing food, but for absorbing carbon dioxide and releasing oxygen in space ships. Having a window to let in the sunlight was found impracticable and an ultra-violet lamp of $7\frac{1}{2}$ kilowatts was designed to illuminate an area of 22 sq. metres. The rate of photosynthesis by algae, however, turned out to be only 25 grams dryweight per sq. metre per day, well below those mentioned for other plants. The space-ship designers eventually concluded[3] that the carbon dioxide could best be removed (though without recovering the oxygen) by the Sabatier process, whereby hydrogen can be made to react with carbon dioxide in the presence of a heated catalyst to produce methane and water.

Let us take as our minimum agricultural require-

[2] Myers, *Aviation Medicine*, August 1954.
[3] Dill & Tamplin, Rand Corporation Publication RM.2542, 1960.

ments the figure worked out in an earlier chapter, of 250 kg. per person per year of grain, vegetables and a few other plants. Let us assume further that the hydrolysis of fibres does not prove satisfactory, or that the fibres are needed for other purposes (making paper for use by the space-ship community, perhaps). Then total requirements will be 500 kg. per person per year or 1375 grams per person per day. If a rate of photosynthesis of 50 grams per square metre per day can be obtained, then—admittedly at austere standards —one person's total agricultural requirements can be obtained from the cultivation, under optimum conditions, of only 27½ sq. metres. Satellites and space ships therefore, with this amount of space reserved on the side facing the sun (or double the area if the satellite is rotating) will be able to provide all the agricultural needs of their inhabitants.

If we are tired of contemplating space travel and residential space ships, let us return to the optimum use of our own earth, and also of the sea. On the former question, an interesting result has recently been published by the Dutch scientist, De Wit, of Wageningen University.[4] He takes almost exactly the same figure as that given above of the gross requirements per person per day of plant dryweight, and also assumes that half of the gross yield of the plant is inedible. He makes the important point that we get the best results by using comparatively tall plants, which are able to spread out for the effective receipt of sunlight an area of leaves much larger than that of the ground on which they stand. The leaves of the

[4] *Harvesting the Sun*, Academic Press, New York and London.

maize plant, for example, even though they shadow each other to some extent, cover five times the area of the ground on which the plant stands. With such plants, and assuming that comparable plants can be developed for colder climates, he put the growth of dry matter per square metre per day (half of which is edible) as high as 68 grams, during periods when the average temperature exceeds 10° C. He goes on to assume that our descendants will have solved the problem of adequately watering all areas, and also of keeping them fully supplied with plant nutrients. Under these circumstances, he plans to make use of the whole 13 billion hectares of the earth's land surface (excluding Greenland and Antarctica).

De Wit's Proposals

Latitude (degrees)	Land surface billion hectares	Number of months in which temperature exceeds 10° C	Edible carbohydrate tons/hectare/ year	People who could be fed at min. standards, billions
70 N	0·8	1	12	10
60 N	1·4	2	21	30
50 N	1·6	6	59	95
40 N	1·5	9	91	136
30 N	1·7	11	113	151
20 N	1·3	12	124	105
10 N	1·0	12	124	77
0	1·4	12	116	121
10 S	0·7	12	117	87
20 S	0·9	12	123	112
30 S	0·7	12	121	88
40 S	0·1	8	89	9
50 S	0·1	1	12	1
TOTAL	13·1			1022

The result came out so large that everyone was surprised, including the author. In these calculations of course no allowance was made for any use of land for residential or recreational purposes. On an alternative assumption that 750 sq. metres per person was reserved for these purposes, the number of persons who could be fed was reduced to 146 billions, even so still a very large figure. However, this is a generous allowance of residential and recreational space. In the new towns recently designed in England the average amount of land per person is 220 sq. metres, and this includes a great deal of open space, playing fields, etc.

De Wit's calculation also assumes that everyone lives close to his food supply. Very considerable economies could be obtained if a large proportion of the population resided in the colder climates, where the sacrifice of agricultural land would have much less effect. This, however, would lead to a gradual transfer of soil mineral nutrients from the land where the food was produced to where it was consumed. So far as nitrogen is concerned, this could easily be made good from the atmosphere, but phosphorus and potash would present greater problems, and might have to be recovered from the sea.

Perhaps, however, our descendants might choose to live in floating palaces at sea, using the land for agriculture. In any case, the calculations of possibilities such as De Wit's will have to be considered (by our descendants) in conjunction with the possibilities of living on space satellites.

A most interesting and entertaining piece of science fiction on this subject (with illustrations) was recently published[5] by Dr Fremlin of Birmingham University. He goes several stages further and assumes that our descendants have mastered artificial photosynthesis, or some other method of synthesising our necessary nutrients. The real limit to the earth's capacity to hold people will be set only by the limits of its capacity to radiate to outer space the heat which they generate. Before this limit is reached, the population of the world could attain a figure with some 16–18 digits in it.

There remain to be examined the possibilities of obtaining food from the sea, and also from lakes, rivers and ponds. It must be remembered that the principal function of fish or other marine products should be not to provide us with our carbohydrates, but with proteins which are not only highly nutritive, but also, unlike leaf proteins, highly palatable. "The sea can be neglected as a source of food," De Wit went so far as to say, "because the amount of minerals that must be added to keep so much water in a reasonable nutritive status is prohibitive." He estimated the rate of photosynthesis by plankton on the surface of the sea at only one-twentieth of the rate of photosynthesis on a land area with comparable climate. The sea plankton enters into large and highly complex "food chains" (i.e. is consumed by one organism which is then consumed by another and so on) ending up with only 1 to 2 per cent of the original weight of plankton taking the form of fish or other marine animals acceptable as human food.

Dr Lucas of the Marine Laboratory at Aberdeen[6]

[5] *New Scientist*, Vol. 24, pp. 285–7.
[6] Results privately communicated.

also estimates the rate of photosynthesis on the surface of the ocean at an average of only 1·8 grams per square metre per day (in rough agreement with De Wit's one-twentieth of the rate on land) or 2 tons per hectare per year, giving 100 billion tons for the whole ocean per year, or 1 to 2 billion tons of edible fish at the end of the food chain.

In fact, phosphorus tends to accumulate in the lower depths of the ocean, and it would be a matter of some difficulty to bring it to the top. However, there are two regions of the ocean where this is done for us naturally, by the upwelling Benguela Current off the west coast of Africa, and by the Humboldt Current off the coast of Peru. In these areas all forms of marine life are much more abundant than elsewhere. The fish catch off the coast of Peru is already being exploited.

Some proposals have recently been put forward for using nuclear power to heat the deep-sea water in the Caribbean Sea, so that the phosphorus-rich water rises to the surface in an area of abundant warmth and sunshine, with consequent expected rapid growth of plankton, and of edible fish.

Some very interesting work is going on in farming fish in ponds in hot climates, where the water is both fertilised, to promote the growth of plant plankton, and further nutrients are added to the water to feed the fish, sometimes agricultural refuse in the shape of husks, stems, etc., and sometimes low-grade cereals. Yields of 2 tons of fish per hectare per year have been attained in a number of cases, and still higher results have been claimed. These are of course a long way below the results which could be obtained in terms of cereals by cultivating dry land of the same area. But fish is very high in protein. This seems an obvious method of remedying protein shortage, at any rate in tropical climates.

One can but conclude with the words of Malcolm Muggeridge, when he said that it seemed strange that such a strong demand for population limitation should come "precisely when the possibilities in the way of food production are seen to be virtually illimitable, and when the whole universe is about to be opened up, providing space to accommodate a million, million times our present squalid little human family".

Recommended Books for Further Reading

General background

Bennett, M. K., *The World's Food*, Harper Bros., New York, 1954.

Chisholm, Michael, *Rural Settlement and Land Use*, Hutchinson, University Library, London, 1966.

Duckham, A. N., *The Farming Year*, Chatto & Windus, London, 1963

FAO, *Agriculture in the world economy*, Rome, 1963.

FAO, *Fisheries in the food economy*, Basic study No. 19, Rome, 1968.

Graham, E. H., *Natural Principles of Land Use*, Oxford University Press, 1944.

Russell, Sir E. John, *World Population and World Food Supplies*, Allen & Unwin, London.

Stamp, D., *Our Undeveloped World*, Faber & Faber, London, 1953. *Man and the Land*, Collins, London.

Agriculture

Gillespie, James & Hathaway, P., *A Textbook of General Agriculture*, Macdonald, London, 1956.

Ministry of Agriculture, Fisheries & Food, *Rations for Livestock*, Bull. No. 48, H.M.S.O., London, 1966.

Watson, J. A. S. & Moore, J. A., *Agriculture*, Oliver & Boyd, Edinburgh, 1962.

Masefield, G. B., *A Handbook of Tropical Agriculture*, Clarendon Press, 1962.

Farm Management

Dexter, Keith & Barber, Derek, *Farming for Profit*, Penguin Books, London, 1961.

Nutrition

Dema, I. S., *Nutrition in Relation to Agricultural Production*, Rome, F.A.O., 1965.

Ministry of Agriculture, Fisheries & Food, *Manual of Nutrition*, H.M.S.O., London, 1966.

Bacharach, A. L., *Science of Nutrition*, Watts, London, 1945.

Population

Clark, Colin, *Population Growth and Land Use*, Macmillan, London, 1967.

Zootechnology

Ovington, J. D. (ed.), *The better use of the World's Fauna for Food*, Symposia of the Institute of Biology, No. 11, Institute of Biology, London, 1963.

Agriculture in Developing Countries

Upton, M. & Antonio, Q. B. O., *Farming as a Business*, Tropical Handbook, Oxford, 1965.

Masefield, G. B., *Famine: its Prevention and Relief*, O.U.P., 1963. *A Short History of Agriculture in the British Colonies*, Clarendon Press, 1950.

Bauer, P. T. & Yamey, B. S., *The Economics of Underdeveloped Countries*, O.U.P., 5th edition, 1963.

Clark, Colin & Haswell, M. R., *The Economics of Subsistence Agriculture*, Macmillan, 3rd edition, 1958.

Irrigation

Clark, Colin, *The Economics of Irrigation*, Pergamon Press, 1967.

I am grateful to Mr K. E. Hunt and Miss M. R. Haswell for help in the compilation of this list.

Index